SULLIVAN

Where did the $13 billion go.

DATE DUE			
DEC 21			

WHERE DID THE $13 BILLION GO?

WHERE DID THE

$13 BILLION GO?

EUGENE SULLIVAN

PRENTICE-HALL, INC.
Englewood Cliffs, N.J.

FOREWORD

At your request I accompany you when you are about your own affairs: my enemies fall upon me and kill me. . . .
You must pay for my death.
You take me to see a wild beast show or that interesting spectacle, a madman; beast or madman kills me. . . .
You must pay.
You hang up your sword; someone else knocks it down so that it cuts me. . . .
You must pay.
In none of these cases can you honestly swear that you did nothing that helped bring about death or wound.

— ANCIENT ANGLO-SAXON LAW

Society has determined that accidents are a price the motorist must pay for the pleasure and convenience of automobile ownership. We permit auto manufacturers to design cars that will satisfy our neurotic appetites. These sleek, low-torsoed, high-horsepowered vehicles are little more than humanized projectiles, capable of causing death and destruction on our nation's highways.

Our representatives legislate severe penalties for traffic violations, knowing that these laws will not be enforced, and more important, that these penalties are only a minor deterrent to hazardous driving practices. In short, we treat the symptoms instead of attacking the disease.

The disease is expensive, as the following items illustrate:

• Motorists paid in excess of $13 billion for auto insurance in 1970.
• Auto insurers paid out approximately $877 million for net economic loss to accident victims in the same year.
• The 1970 highway toll reached approximately 22,133,-000 accidents with 55,400 deaths and 4,950,000 injuries.

- These accidents resulted in a loss of $16 billion to the nation's economy.

Recognizing the need for reform in the insurance industry, New York Governor Nelson A. Rockefeller in 1967 appointed a Governor's Committee on Compensating Victims of Automobile Accidents. In his message to the committee the governor said:

"Our present tort liability system for compensating the victims of automobile accidents has been authoritatively criticized as slow, expensive, and unfair. The system has remained essentially unchanged while the nation has passed from the horse-and-buggy era to an age dominated by the automobile—with the highway accident an all-too-common occurrence.

"The time has come for a thorough study of how automobile victims are affected by the lengthy and difficult process of determining fault and resolving claims following automobile accidents, with a view to possible changes in the system."

Unless the present insurance system is changed drastically and soon, these figures will continue to rise. At best, we can look forward to the following in 1971 and 1972:

- One out of every four drivers will have an accident.
- One out of every four accident victims will receive absolutely nothing from their auto-insurance companies.
- Victims with severe injuries—those who do collect—will receive an average of only 30 percent of their net economic loss.
- Lawyers will pocket about half of their income from accident victims—an amount close to $1 billion.
- Insurance agents will collect over $726 million in commissions for selling auto insurance.
- Thousands of motorists will have their auto-insurance policies cancelled.
- Thousands more will be forced to pay exorbitant premiums as a result of being placed in assigned-risk plans.

YOU MUST PAY

If we can accept all of this, if we can accept the death and destruction, the injuries and the suffering caused by the automobiles in our society, then we must make every effort to make these burdens tolerable. This means that traffic engineering, road design, auto manufacturers, and law enforcement will have to become meaningful and efficient to meet today's motoring needs. It means, too, that auto insurers will have to accept their full responsibility.

Our present insurance system is archaic, obsolescent, and untrustworthy. It feeds upon the gullibility, ignorance, and permissiveness of the motoring public. Auto insurance is becoming more difficult to obtain and even harder to keep.

The time has come—indeed, it is long overdue—that we look at the entire automobile-insurance situation for ourselves. We, the motoring public, must decide what we want in an insurance system. It is hoped that this book will assist in that determination.

E. S.

New York City

CONTENTS

PART I

THE AUTOMOBILE
INSURANCE INDUSTRY

THE PRICE TAG

In the United States today over 52 million policyholders spend $13 billion annually to insure 100 million passenger automobiles.

The insurers and courts, combined with state legislatures, state insurance departments, attorneys, adjusters, and policyholders, make up an insurance establishment that is in serious difficulty.

The insurance industry for the past two decades has steadily increased rates while reducing insurance availability. It has become inhuman, unjust, inconsiderate, and irresponsible toward policyholders. It has failed to upgrade its services and responsibilities to the motoring public. Its nationwide lobby system meanwhile has been extremely active in securing passage of special-interest legislation. Much of this legislation has resulted in tremendous profits without regard for the needs of those it purports to protect.

As we shall see, the current efforts by the insurance lobby are directed toward nullifying reform efforts. These lobbies, in league with the legal profession, have seriously impaired attempts to provide faster and more equitable compensation to accident victims.

Passenger cars are increasing at the rate of three and a half million a year. The federal government has spent billions on the interstate-highway network, enabling drivers to travel across the country without stopping for a traffic light. Yet driving in any of our cities is a nightmare.

Some within the system recognize that there are problems, but most of these people would like to see change come as quietly as possible and be spread out over many years. Most do not want the system to change in any of its fundamental characteristics. The motoring public has the most to gain or lose under any system. What does it want?

A recent Department of Transportation study showed that an overwhelming majority of motorists would like to see a better system. At present, court delays in settling claims of up to five years are not uncommon. The failure of state insurance departments to regulate the insurers effectively is evidenced by the number of bankrupt companies and the hundreds of thousands of claimants and policyholders they have left to face financial hardships. What are we really buying from the insurers? Where did the $13 billion go?

THE PRICE TAG

Bodily Injury Liability	$6,050,000,000
Property Damage Liability	2,655,500,000
*Auto Physical Damage and Miscellaneous	4,845,000,000
	$13,550,500,000

*Includes fire, theft, collision, medical, and uninsured motorist coverages.

Since we are primarily interested in bodily-injury liability insurance, our analysis of premium dollars will be confined to that area. The total bodily-injury premium is broken down as follows:

4

BODILY-INJURY PREMIUM — 1970

$6,050,000,000

Insurers' administrative costs and agents' commissions	$1,997 million
Lawyers (both plaintiff and defense) and adjusters	1,392 million
Total operating costs (equal to 56% of premium)	$3,389 million

The remaining 44 percent of the premium dollar is apportioned as follows:

Duplication of benefits	$ 484 million
General damages (pain and suffering)	1,300 million
Amount paid to claimants for net economic loss	877 million
Total	$6,050 million

Out of the $6 billion in premiums, the insurers paid out only *$877 million* to accident victims for net economic loss.

The first item of almost $2 billion for the agents' commissions and insurers' administrative costs is a considerable one. Most independent agents average 15 percent of premium as a commission, but when we group all agents' costs, we must allow for the direct writers. This brings our average down to 12 percent, or $726 million, for the agents. The administrative costs, which include general expenses, taxes, profits, advertising, and the like, cost 21 percent of the premium dollar, or $1,271 million. We can assume that these administrative costs are as low as the insurers want them to be, or as high as they can get away with. However, the $726 million to agents is another matter. When we reflect on the significance of this figure, we see that a difference of only $151 million separates the amount of money claimants receive for net economic loss and the commissions paid agents. Can anyone but an agent justify such a ridiculous set of circumstances? Just what services do agents perform that would allow them such a disproportionate share of the premium dollar? The answer is that they perform very little indeed. But under the present auto-insurance system, motorists have few choices other than the agency system from which to purchase insurance. We will discuss the agents' role further in another chapter.

Lawyers and adjusters absorb another $1.4 billion of the premium dollar. The adjuster's role is obvious: he is there to safeguard the insurers' interests. Lawyers, of course, present a major problem. The present insurance system virtually subsidizes the fraternity of trial lawyers. It may well be true that, without lawyers, some claimants would receive less in settlements than they are entitled to, but it is also true that whatever the claimant receives, a percentage of this goes to pay for the services of the lawyer. Quite often, in fact, the claimant would end up with more money if he did not engage the services of a lawyer.

Collateral sources of accident benefits are another drain on the premium dollar. In 1970, $484 million was paid to claimants for medical and wage losses that had already been paid by other sources, such as Blue Cross. This duplication of benefits is costly, and in some instances it is unnecessary.

Pain and suffering, or general damages, in the amount of $1.3 billion was given away, for the most part, to victims of minor accidents with minor injuries or no injuries at all. If these awards for pain and suffering had been paid to the seriously injured, so that all of the victims' medical and wage losses, even future losses, were paid, then there could possibly be some justification for these payments under the present system.

The last item of $877 million is the amount paid to claimants for their medical and wage loss expenses in that year. As we can see, the money the insurers gave away in the form of pain and suffering is almost one and a half times the amount paid to cover economic losses. The comparison of the total paid bodily-injury premium of $6 billion to a miserly payout of $877 million for net economic loss is stultifying. The federal government, with all of its bureaucracy, manages to return through the Social Security Administration, 95 cents to the public for every $1 paid in. It costs the policyholder approximately $6 for every $1 received in net-economic-loss benefits from the insurers.

Figures and statistics alone do not tell the stories of hardship, suffering, and deprivation that policyholders and claimants have been subjected to as a result of the present insurance system. The following three case histories are examples in point:

In South Carolina, a young sailor just home from Vietnam received notice from his insurance company that his policy had been canceled. The sailor wrote and asked the company why his auto insurance had been canceled. The insurer replied:

> This letter is in response to your inquiry regarding the reasons for our decision to cancel your automobile insurance policy. Investigation revealed that your wife has a bad moral reputation and is an excessive user of intoxicants. I hope that this will be a satisfactory answer to your questions.

The smugness, impropriety, and callousness of this letter is inexcusable. To a sailor just home from Vietnam, married to a pretty wife and the father of two young children, a letter of this sort could have disastrous effects—not the least of which would be to break up the young man's home.

The sailor quickly appealed to the South Carolina insurance department, and they answered that, even though the insurer could not substantiate these allegations, the com-

7

pany was perfectly within its rights under the law, and there was nothing that could be done about it. The young wife went to an attorney and tried to bring a libel action against the insurer. The lawyer informed the girl that under South Carolina laws the insurance companies are not liable for any statement made to policyholders when this statement concerns the cancellation of insurance. Although the action by the state insurance department legally cleared the young lady, the insurer refused to insure the couple. When they applied to other companies, they were refused insurance because of the cancellation. Finally they were forced into the assigned-risk market and had to pay a premium of $395 a year, which was double their previous premium of $176.

The young woman's attorney in his investigation found that she had never been arrested for any reason, that she had never had a traffic violation, and that as far as he could determine, her character was exemplary. The state insurance department investigated the insurer's allegations and could find no basis for cancellation, and in fact, could not even bring the matter to a hearing. The young woman stands condemned by the insurance community. In every case where the young couple tried to get standard insurance, reason for the prior insurer's cancellation had to be given. "It's so humiliating to tell these people why I have been canceled," she says. "I always have to explain."

Here is a situation where the investigator for the insurance company probably exaggerated what he had learned as hearsay. Undoubtedly, the investigator had not turned in his quota of dirt and had to manufacture some of his own. The real problem here is the relative impunity with which an insurer is able to make unsupported allegations concerning an insured's private life. There have been many movies made about the innocent man imprisoned or sent to the electric chair for a crime he did not commit. Our sensibilities are outraged at this sort of injustice. No human being wants to be accused of anything unjustly; but, worse than that, when the accuser can make allegations without being required to prove them, human rights are seriously violated. What is wrong with states like South Carolina that have legislated these protective laws for their insurers? This sort of thing can happen to anyone. Very few motorists who apply for insurance are not investigated by the insurers. Who will investigate the investigators? What if credit-card companies, department stores, and the like were given the same privilege of immunity as the insurers? Any person could be forced into second-rate citizenship, complete with all of the attendant ugly rumors which could force a person out of his community. Are we going to allow the insurers to become "Big Brother"?

Then there is the case of the Christophers. Albert and Susan Christopher,* in July of 1967, started out on their first vacation in years. They left their two children with Albert's parents in Hartford, Connecticut, and drove all the first day, reaching the Pennsylvania line by late afternoon, where they stopped at a motel. Susan was an editor for a Hartford newspaper, and she planned to write a series of articles on Civil War battlegrounds. Albert was an engineer for a local construction firm. At six o'clock the following morning, they left the motel and drove off down a three-lane country road which connected with the interstate highway some ten miles further along. They fell in behind a pickup truck and waited for the lane markings to allow them to pass. When Albert saw that he could pass safely, he inched out into the center lane and proceeded to pass the truck. As he came abreast of the truck, he saw a car approaching from the opposite direction, also in the center lane. Albert glanced to his right and saw that the

---

*All names have been changed to protect the privacy of the individuals involved.

truck driver was keeping up with him. The driver was not watching the road, but was staring down into the car at Susan. Albert honked his horn, pushed the accelerator to the floor, and shot ahead. During the time Albert had gone into the passing lane, another car had moved up behind the truck, making it impossible for Albert to fall back safely. When he saw that he had no choice but to cut into the right lane in front of the truck, the oncoming car seemed inches away. Albert hooked his rear fender on the bumper of the truck, losing control of the car. The car overturned and skidded across the road into the oncoming car.

The Christophers were taken to the county hospital in an ambulance. Susan, only 30 years old, suffered a compression fracture with spinal-cord compression followed by paraplegia. Albert, 33, had an impacted fracture of the spine with no permanency. Both suffered other injuries. Albert was released from the hospital after three weeks. Susan was not so fortunate; it was more than nine months before she was released and then in a wheelchair to which she would be confined for the rest of her life. In addition to the anguish she suffered as a result of the accident, she was not able to see her children, which caused deep depression. In the three years between the accident and the trial, the Christophers accrued $14,000 in medical expenses and another $25,000 in lost wages for a total of $39,000.

At the trial, the Christophers' attorney rested his defense on the negligence of the truck driver and the other driver. It was, however, impossible to prove. The truck driver's attorney moved that the Christophers had not made a prima facie case. The judge granted the motion, and the trial was over. There were no injuries to the driver of the car the Christophers' vehicle collided with and no case made by the driver. Albert wheeled his wife from the courtroom with tears streaming down his face. For three years, they had lived in apprehension, waiting for the trial.

10

Now, in a flash, it was over, and nothing was paid by the insurance company.

A year after the accident, Albert, Susan, and the children had to move in with his parents. In order to meet their medical expenses their house was sold. The sale netted $2,000, which they promptly applied to their medical bill. Their hospitalization coverage had paid $4,200 of the expense, leaving them a balance owed of $7,800. Susan will be under a doctor's care for the rest of her life, and even if there had been a chance of rehabilitation for her, the family finances would not have allowed it.

The Christophers' case is typical of many. The complete and utter failure of the present insurance system to compensate accident victims for their wage and medical losses is deplorable and morally indefensible.

John Fillmore is 47 years old, black, and the father of six children. He is uneducated and for the last 24 years has worked as a porter for a rug-cleaning company. In 1964, John was forced to move his family, due to an urban-renewal project. The city found a place large enough for John and his family, but it was on the other side of town. John was forced to buy a car. Because he was black, lived in a ghetto area, and had limited driving experience, he was forced into the high-risk insurance market. He had to finance his auto-insurance premium of $590 at usurious rates with his insurance agent.

The agent placed him with a company only two years old, which we will call the Acme Mutual Insurance Company. John was with the company for one year and the following year was able to place his insurance with a standard insurer. In 1968, Mr. Fillmore received an assessment of $389 from Acme Mutual, which had declared that it was insolvent. Mr. Fillmore found that the $389 was more than he could borrow. He was forced to sell his television set and a few other household items to pay the assessment.

11

Mr. Fillmore is a proud man, and it can be imagined that explaining the missing television set to six youngsters was no easy job.

The management of Acme Mutual, of course, was guilty of fraud, mismanagement, and outright thievery. The insurance agent cared only for the 30 percent commission, or $196, plus his high interest rates in financing John's auto insurance.

We will go into cases of this sort in greater detail in later chapters. The issue here is what policyholders are getting for their money. It is obvious that, if there are a great many cases like the foregoing, the motoring public is getting very little. Unfortunately, this is the case. Hundreds of thousands of accident victims can attest to this, as can the thousands of policyholders victimized by insolvent insurers.

We have spoken of the insurers generally, but who are they? What are they? Why do they take advantage of the public? We hope to be able to provide insights into the whys as we move through this book. The first step is to identify and explain just what the insurance establishment is comprised of and how it operates.

The establishment is made up of 858 companies, many of which write other forms of insurance in addition to auto lines. The 858 companies are broken down into four major classifications according to their structure. These classifications follow:

1. Stock companies
2. Mutual companies
3. Reciprocal exchanges
4. Lloyds underwriters

STOCK COMPANIES

The term "stock company" means that a corporation has issued shares of stock (ownership) in the company. Most commonly, these shares are offered to the public at a price which is dependent on such factors as expected profitability or company growth. The investors look forward to yearly dividends and capital gains appreciation for the use of their money by the company. A stock insurance company is similar to any other company in these respects, but it has additional responsibilities. An insurer must have a charter and allow itself to be regulated by the insurance department in any state within which it intends to do business. The federal government also has laws with which the insurers must comply though insurance operations are free from federal government regulations.

One of the primary requirements of each state is that an insurer must have adequate capital and surplus funds for each line of insurance to be sold. For instance, in one state an insurer offering bodily-injury coverage must have a minimum capital fund of perhaps $100,000 and a surplus fund of another $50,000. The insurer can only issue policies in relation to its surplus. If a company wanted to offer property damage or comprehensive insurance, it would have to provide additional statutory surplus amounts for each kind of insurance. The capital funds are not considered by the state insurance departments as surplus with which to write policies. Most insurance-company stocks are traded on the over-the-counter market, but some are listed on the New York and American stock exchanges as well.

According to the *National Underwriter*, an insurance trade paper, there were 574 stock companies, which wrote almost $8 billion in earned premiums in 1969. These companies represented 60 percent of the total auto insurance sold for that year. The foremost stock insurer is

Allstate Insurance Company, a subsidiary of Sears-Roebuck, which is followed by Aetna Life and Casualty and the Travelers Insurance Company. Allstate is also the second largest auto insurer in the country, with premiums that passed the $1 billion mark for the first time in 1969. The company is also an independent in that it does not subscribe to any rating organizations, but sets its own rates. The company claims that it offers the policyholder savings of as much as 17 percent over regular bureau rates. A recent report from a consumer's union, published by *Consumer Reports*, rated Allstate as being poorer than average in claims handling, of having a much higher incidence of policy cancellations than average, and of having big step-ups in its rates. Aetna and Travelers are not much better in their overall dealings with policyholders either, according to the same report, and they have the added disadvantage of using the independent-agency system, which adds unnecessary expense to their insurance costs.

The major problem with the stock companies is that they have a primary responsibility to their stockholders, which must come before consideration for policyholders. The companies spend a great deal of money through public relations and advertising to convince us differently, but the evidence plainly favors the stockholder over the policyholder. Raising rates to policyholders and at the same time increasing dividends to stockholders is certainly evidence enough of this partiality.

MUTUAL COMPANIES

The mutual form of insurance company is a corporation also and like a stock company is subject to rules and regulations set by the states. Unlike a stock company, a mutual is owned by the policyholders. With the purchase of an auto-insurance policy, and in some instances the payment of a nominal membership fee, the insurance purchaser becomes part owner of the mutual company. Theoretically and depending upon the bylaws of the company, at any point in time, a majority of the policyholders can vote to dissolve the company and to divide its assets among the policyholders (owners). Today some mutuals pay annual dividends to policyholders at the end of the policy year. In others the dividend is anticipated and the premium is reduced by the equivalency of the dividend. But in the main, the dividend is a thing of the past. Competition has become fierce, and mere survival for many of these companies is the first consideration.

There are two principal types of mutuals dealing in auto insurance. The first is the assessment mutual, which can issue policies of contingent liability. The contingent-liability policy is a device whereby a newly formed mutual can protect itself from paying out all of its surplus funds in the event of a bad underwriting year. If a company had a bad underwriting year, the total loss could be divided by the number of policyholders, and each would be liable for that amount. Usually the maximum assessment is fixed by the states at no more than one year's premium. The number of assessable mutuals is declining rapidly.

The second type of mutual is the nonassessable mutual. State laws allow that, when a mutual has a surplus fund matching the minimum requirements of the state, it may issue nonassessable policies.

The mutuals are increasing their share of the auto-insurance market yearly. In 1969, 255 mutuals wrote 31.8 percent of all auto premiums.

The largest auto insurer in the country is State Farm Mutual; with premiums of over $1.5 billion in 1969, it is far ahead of its closest competitor, Allstate Insurance Company. Unlike Allstate, State Farm is regarded as one of the finest insurance companies in the country, according to *Consumer Reports*. Its claims-handling procedure is far above average, and its incidence of policy cancellations is much lower than average. State Farm's rates are generally lower than those of most companies, and in most states it offers savings of up to 30 percent over its competitors. Liberty Mutual, a Boston-based auto insurer, is also noted for being an excellent company.

RECIPROCAL EXCHANGES

The reciprocal exchange is an American innovation which had its start back in the late nineteenth century. The reciprocal is an unincorporated system whereby persons join together and agree to exchange private contracts of indemnity—insure each other—at a relatively low cost. An exchange does not issue policies; it merely provides a system for the exchange of indemnification. Each subscriber to the system becomes a partner in the insurance business and assumes his proportionate share of the risks and profits. The exchange is managed by an attorney-in-fact who is paid a percentage of the premiums received. The attorney-in-fact can be a corporation or an individual. The subscribers also may choose an advisory board to supervise the attorney-in-fact as well as other aspects of the exchange's operations. Generally, the reciprocals are less closely regulated than stock and mutual companies. The reciprocals are few in number, based mainly in southern California. In 1969 they accounted for 7.6 percent of the total auto-premium market, together with Lloyds groups.

The leading reciprocal insurer is Farmer's Exchange, based in Los Angeles, California, where it writes most of its business. This exchange was rated as the No. 7 auto insurer in the country in 1969, with an annual premium that year of $298 million. The leading reciprocal, however, in terms of services, is United Services Automobile Association of San Antonio, Texas. This company sells via the mails to commissioned officers in the military and is rated as second only to State Farm Mutual in service.

LLOYDS UNDERWRITERS

Lloyds of London and American Lloyds are not insurance companies, but groups of individual underwriters. Their significance in this country is minimal. London Lloyds, however, is the largest reinsurer in the world.

INSURANCE OPERATIONS

Irrespective of the form of company, be it mutual, stock, or reciprocal exchange, the day-to-day operations of each are quite similar: insurance must be sold, underwritten, priced; claims must be processed, investigated, and paid; and surplus and unearned premium reserves must be invested.

In order to market insurance, a philosophy must be decided upon. This philosophy might be better customer service, discounts for compact cars, or simply lower prices. Whatever the philosophy, and whether it is meaningful or not, it is offered as a lure to the prospective insurance buyer. The marketing of insurance is for some firms a serious matter. Those firms specializing in mail order, or those which depend on their own exclusive agents to bring in business, must have a viable service to sell. Usually it is lower prices.

The mail-order companies have been exceptionally successful in recent years in selling auto insurance. Their good fortune is that they do not have to pay substantial commissions to agents, which can run as high as 15 percent on each policy sold by the companies using the agency system. These savings are passed on to the insurance buyer in the form of lower premiums.

The so-called direct writers—State Farm Mutual, Allstate—rely upon their own employees to market and service their customers locally. The savings to these companies can be more than 10 percent when using their own salaried personnel. Companies using the American agency system have to rely on independent service firms to handle their servicing requirements. If these companies are to compete, they have to offer something to their customers other than price. More often than not, anything they do offer is meaningless.

The claim of these companies that their agents offer services the public needs is exaggerated. An agent's fee is usually 15 percent of the paid-in premium, and often an extra fee for handling the routine policy applications is collected from the applicant as well. It is inconceivable that the agent is worth this. Unfortunately, the majority of insurers use the agency system, and the motoring public must subsidize its existence. All of these companies—direct writers, agency, and mail-order writers—advertise their philosophies, and if their techniques are successful, they will have a large group of applicants from which to select the most desirable risks.

Under the present system, the underwriting function is the very basis for a company's survival. If a company accepts too many bad risks, it can have an unfavorable loss experience or even a disastrous loss, forcing it into insolvency. The companies set up guidelines under which an applicant will be deemed acceptable. These guidelines vary with each company, but factors such as age, race, color, occupation, place of residence, and personal habits can determine an applicant's insurability. A clergyman, for instance, is a bad risk, because he is often occupied with church problems at all hours of the day and night, and because he thinks about these problems and is preoccupied with them, he is likely to have an accident.

Applicants who have been refused insurance from the standard insurers are allowed to apply to the assigned-risk pools in their states. In these pools motorists are often required to pay higher premiums. All too frequently, the assigned-risk market will not accept certain applicants because of premium-financing restrictions; they are then forced into purchasing insurance from substandard insurers. The rates charged by these companies are often extremely high. It is not unusual to find applicants paying up to 500 percent over standard rates in order to obtain insurance.

The majority of these applicants are "clean risks" who just happen to live in ghetto areas or have limited experience. In the daily operations of an insurance company, the underwriters match applicants against company guidelines, and the actual pricing is based upon experience and projections calculated by the firms' actuaries or often the rates published by rating bureaus.

The claims received by an insurer are processed and are usually investigated by adjusters. The results of the investigation lead to a value for the claim. To this value the company must add overhead and attorneys' and adjusters' expenses. The total of all of these is called loss and loss adjustment expense. Most of this expense is allowed to make money for the insurer as it stays in the investment portfolio until the insurer is forced to pay the claim.

The tremendous amounts of premium dollars, $13.5 billion in 1970 less agents' fees, plus surplus and contingency reserve funds, are all invested in various securities and real estate. Counselors for the insurers research and direct all of these security investments in what is called an investment portfolio. The state insurance commissions regulate the kinds and amounts of investments a company may make. Profits are enormous and are of more importance to the insurers than their underwriting experience under normal loss situations. When the underwriting shows a profit as well, the overall profitability can be appreciable.

It could well be that insurers would rather make most of their profits through investments. The federal tax on capital gains, of 25 percent, is substantially less than the 48 percent paid on underwriting profits.

DIFFERENCES BETWEEN STOCK AND MUTUAL INSURERS

One of the basic differences between the stock and the mutual insurer is the question of responsibility to the insured. The stock company is owned by the stockholders, and the performance of a stock insurer is measured by the size and dependability of dividends as well as future profit potential. This performance is reflected in the price of the stock. Therefore, the primary responsibility of the stock insurer is to the stockholders and not to the policyholders. The overwhelming majority of policyholders are not stockholders and look to their insurers to provide them with services that are prompt and dependable.

The premiums which an insurer accepts from its policyholders are fiduciary in nature. That is, the insurer holds these funds as a sort of trust for the insurable period. These funds do not belong to the insurer until they are earned, and while they are held, the funds are invested and earn profits for the insurer. Portions of these earnings are placed in surplus, reinvested, used to pay for any underwriting losses, or paid to stockholders in the form of dividends. Each policyholder, then, becomes an investor in the future of the insurer. This relationship implies a responsibility, above all other considerations, to the policyholder. In actual practice this responsibility is denied by the insurers, and the surpluses grow, dividends to stockholders are increased, while the policyholders and claimants suffer rate increases, policy cancellations, and poor reparative procedures involving partial payment or no payment at all.

The fiduciary aspect, however, should not be allowed to confuse the true relationship between investment income, income from the unearned premium reserve, and any other income. The fact is that all income belongs to the company, and the company *is* its management, its stockholders, and its policyholders. No part of the company should receive any special financial consideration to the detriment of other parts of the company. Therefore, the management must make provision for future growth, the stockholders should receive a dividend for the use of their money, and the policyholder should see his rate increase or decrease as a result of the *total* profitability of the company. The term "fiduciary" should perhaps only be understood in the context that, should a policyholder cancel his policy, his prepaid premium is safe and will be returned to him.

There are other complex considerations regarding the term "fiduciary" as it relates to the business of insurance, and some of these are discussed in other sections of this book.

In the ten-year period ending in 1968 auto-insurance company gains from stockholders' equity, underwriting, and assets increased by $4.7 billion. It would appear that this increase was made at great expense to the policyholders.

In addition, the stock companies have become prizes for

acquisition-minded conglomerates. The sizable assets of these insurers, created by policyholders and to a far lesser degree by stockholders, are desperately needed by the cash-hungry conglomerates. We will look into this situation in detail in a later chapter. Suffice to say that, as usual, the victims are the policyholders.

The mutual auto insurer is owned by the policyholders, and in theory at least, this would obviate the problem of stockholder involvement. At this point, perhaps a brief history of the mutual insurer is in order.

On February 18, 1752, Benjamin Franklin founded the first insurance company in North America. The Philadelphia Contributorship for the Insurance of Houses from Loss by Fire was formed around the concept of mutual risk, whereby every man might help another without any disservice to himself. The Contributorship is still in the business of insuring houses from loss by fire after 218 years of uninterrupted service to its policyholders. Since 1895 the company has paid an annual dividend of 10 percent on all policies that have been in effect for ten years or longer. The company is so strong financially that a premium of only 2 percent of the insured value is paid once, and the policy is in force for perpetuity. Thus, if a home was insured for $20,000 in 1950 with a payment of $400, starting in 1960, a dividend of $40 would be paid that year and every succeeding year. The policyholder would have collected $400 in dividends by 1970. If a policyholder elected to cancel the policy, the original payment of $400 would be returned to him.

The Automobile Mutual Insurance Company of America, formed in Providence, Rhode Island, in 1907, was the first mutual insurer to provide coverage for motorists. This company has been insuring selected risks for 63 years and is currently paying a dividend of 35 percent of premium to policyholders. The company was formed by a group of

Rhode Island businessmen, and at the end of its first year of operations was able to return a dividend of 25 percent to policyholders. The company writes only auto comprehensive insurance. In 1921, a companion firm, Factory Mutual Liability Insurance Company, was formed to provide all auto liability lines of insurance. The company has paid an annual dividend of not less than 25 percent since its founding to its policyholders. In 1969, this firm earned premiums of $39 million. The Factory Mutual, like its parent firm, offers only selected-risk insurance. Neither company has salesmen or agents; all business is solicited through the mails.

These companies, and there are several more, best exemplify the mutual concept. The small mutual can cater to the needs of a select group within a state or even in several states with a great degree of efficiency. The policyholders, being an integral part of their company, are more aware of their company and can direct their concern over management decisions effectively. The large mutuals have had to forgo this intimacy with the policyholders because of their sheer size. It is demonstrably evident that these mutuals have actively and conscientiously fulfilled their role as insurers. The motoring public's needs for insurance increase at some 4 percent a year, or approximately 3.5 million private passenger cars yearly. In 1958, State Farm and its affiliate absorbed 1.2 million of these new insureds. This is surely a fine testimony to State Farm's social responsibility. Most of the stock companies tightened up their underwriting, and the resultant spate of cancellations and nonrenewals encouraged the fly-by-night, high-risk operators to set up shop and milk the motorists. But the mutuals see their potential for insurance decreasing in the coming years.

State laws require that an insurer accept a premium volume that is in a direct and safe relationship to its surplus. The mutual insurer cannot go into the money markets and borrow; it must rely upon its own resources, which are investment income and policyholders' premiums, to allow its surplus to grow. Of course, the large mutuals could forget their responsibility and refuse to accept new policyholders. If this were to happen, the present insurance crisis would become a catastrophe.

The stock companies, on the other hand, are paying out their dividends to stockholders, restricting their underwriting, and building up huge surpluses. These huge surpluses in turn become prizes for the conglomerates, which acquire the insurer and use the surplus for other purposes.

Another game the stock insurers are playing is called the formation of holding companies. These holding companies are financed through the insurer's surplus funds, causing a further depletion of the insurer's capacity to insure. Many states have recognized this problem and are establishing regulations for mergers and acquisitions that will protect the policyholders and the general public.

There are 20 auto-insurance companies at the top of the establishment. These 20 companies are responsible for more than 50 percent of all the auto insurance written in the country. Many of these insurers are just divisions of even larger corporate giants with interests in many fields. Of the 20, only four are mutuals, three are reciprocals, and the remaining 13 are stock companies.

The political power of these companies is awesome. In every state and in Washington, lobbyists in the pay of the insurers fight to preserve the status quo. The majority of the insurers do not want any changes in the system unless it benefits them. To safeguard their interests effectively, the National Association of Life Underwriters has even published a booklet on how to influence legislators. One of the interesting facets of this booklet, entitled *State Legislation Actions,* is a set of instructions on how to prepare a dossier on each legislator. The booklet recommends that the legislators' insurance company be ascertained, if he has any relatives in the insurance business, if he has any close personal friends in the insurance business, and who might be the person most able to influence him. The legislator's lawyer and banking relationships are also investigated. It is difficult to condone the propriety of such methods of influencing legislation favorable to the insurers. In some ways it is almost frightening. It is doubtful that any consumer organization could muster a fraction of the power used by the insurers in fighting for their rights.

Another aspect of the power is seldom recognized: that is, the trust of the policyholder. For many years, motorists have been placing their insurance with the same companies and have considered themselves to be part of the companies. Some will even speak proudly of the fact that they have been driving for 15 or 20 years without ever having to submit a claim to their insurers. These people do not know and would not believe that their insurers would do anything to them that would not be in their best interests. There are millions of motorists in this category. It is only when they have an accident or their policies are canceled because of age or for some other reason that they find out the true attitudes of the insurers.

There are times when it seems the stock insurers have deliberately created chaos in order to force the federal government into the insurance business. This will certainly happen at some point in the future, and it will probably be a good thing. However, there are problems enough without adding conjecture to the list. Much of the current controversy over the insurers is concerned with their profitability; the next chapter deals with stock and mutual company profits.

STOCK COMPANY PROFITS

The automobile insurers have two primary sources of profits: investments and underwriting. The bulk of the insurers' surplus and reserve funds are invested in the stocks and bonds of many businesses, and in bonds and notes of state and federal governments. The investment program of an insurer is called its investment portfolio. State insurance departments restrict the amount of common stock in a portfolio to an amount guaranteeing solvency to the best of their regulating ability, regardless of normal stock-market fluctuations. Further restrictions are imposed upon the amount of stock that can be owned by an insurer in any one corporation.

In addition to these restrictions, others require an insurer to invest a minimum amount in state and municipal bonds within the state in which it operates.

Insurers operating in several states are required to meet the insurance-investment laws of each state. The stock insurers' surplus and reserve funds are composed of capital funds, regular surplus (which is the difference between assets and liabilities), loss adjustment reserves (which are claims in process, or unreported, but not paid), and any special contingency reserves such as reserves for catastrophic loss. All of these funds are invested and return profits in four ways: interest, dividends paid on investments in corporations, capital gains realized through the sale of stock at a price higher than its original costs, and unrealized capital gains, which is the appreciated value carried as an asset but not sold to realize that value.

Insurers often have real-estate holdings that provide income through rents and, in addition, provide increased asset value through land and building appreciation. This income is of small significance, because real-estate holdings are restricted by law in most states

The object of state investment restrictions is to safeguard the insurers' ability to pay claims promptly. An insurer must be able to convert securities into cash quickly. Real estate is not a readily negotiable asset. Common stocks are also subject to wide fluctuations in value, and an insurer which speculated heavily in the stock market, under certain adverse conditions, could face ruin. Corporate bonds, municipal bonds, and federal treasury notes, however, are quickly negotiable.

Underwriting *is* the business of insurance. The auto insurer agrees to indemnify (protect) a policyholder against possible financial loss, under bodily-injury and property-damage insurance coverage, from claims by a third party. Other coverages on a first-party basis—the insurer pays the policyholder directly—are collision, comprehensive, and uninsured-motorist protection. The process of risk selection for three coverages in an insurance policy is called underwriting.

All insurers hope to make profits from their underwriting. These profits are calculated as the difference between loss, loss-adjustment expenses, acquisition costs, taxes, general overhead, and earned premiums. The term "loss-adjustment expense" is the sum of legal and adjusters' fees and other expenses. The term "earned premium" is essential to understanding the insurance business.

The prepayment of premiums represents a deferred liability to the insurer over the life of an insurance policy. At any point during the insured period, the policyholder has the right to cancel. If he does, the unearned portion of the premium must be returned to him. For example, if the insured paid a premium of $120 for a 12-month policy, the company can only claim a portion, one twelfth each month, or $10 per month. If a company canceled his policy in the third month, the company would have earned $30, and the rebate to the policyholder would be $90.

Another way of saying this is that the $30 represents the earned premium and the $90 the unearned premium. Therefore, when an insurer calculates its yearly underwriting experience (profit or loss), it measures the loss and loss-adjustment expenses paid to claimants against the earned premium. The result is expressed as the ratio between the two. For instance, in 1969, all stock companies reported an average loss ratio of 62.4 percent. The general operating expenses of the company, such as agents' commissions, overhead, and advertising, must be added to the loss ratio. This combined ratio, of course, varies with each company. Thus, if the combined loss and expense ratio is under 100 percent, the insurer is earning a profit; if over, it is losing money.

Scarcely a month passes that we do not read an article concerning the "staggering" losses of the auto insurers. True, some of the auto insurers are losing money, but only in their underwriting. The investment side of the business is returning substantial profits. Why the auto insurers are continually claiming financial distress is understandable: it would be difficult for them to justify their annual rate increases if they did not understate their true financial position.

On August 10, 1970, the *Wall Street Journal* reported: "Travelers Corp., Hartford . . . said its underwriting losses narrowed to $16 million in the first six months of this year from a $33 million loss a year earlier. The smaller loss enabled Travelers to report adjusted net income of $40.2 million, or 85 cents a share, up from $33.1 million, or 69 cents a share, a year before. . . ."

To the layman, it must be strange indeed when a company can report that a smaller year-end *loss* enabled them to report a larger profit. How can an insurer lose money and make a profit? The fact is that the insurers are sound financially. The total gain from operations and investments for the auto insurers during the period 1957-1968 amounted to $6.1 billion! In those same years the "staggering" underwriting losses came to a mere $1.4 billion. The real answer to the dilemma is that the insurers have a unique financial reporting system. They use only part of their business to indicate profitability.

While there is no excuse for the emphasis that auto insurers place on underwriting results in reporting profitability, it must be explained that there are two methods of reporting the financial condition of a stock insurance company.

Each year, state insurance departments require insurers to submit a statutory analysis, called a convention report. This report contains financial information from which the state determines the solvency of each insurer. In addition, the report contains underwriting results. In most states, investment income is not a factor in determining the profitability of the stock insurer. The states are primarily concerned that an insurer is solvent and that the insurer has realistically evaluated its loss reserves and unearned premium reserves. This report is used by the insurers, if they have experienced an adverse underwriting year, to back up their requests for rate increases. And some states allow increases based upon this report alone, without taking into account that the companies might actually have had the most profitable year in the history of auto insurance!

One of the main controversies over the use of the convention report is centered around an accounting principle. Under the statutory system of accounting, commissions, processing, and other initial expenses are charged off when incurred rather than being treated as a prepaid expense and shown on the balance sheet as an asset. As we indicated earlier, an insurer can only claim the earned premium as income even though the full premium is collected in advance from the policyholder. Thus, if a company wrote

$100,000 in premiums, all the expenses generated by these premiums would have to be taken from the surplus account, because the company would not yet have earned any of the premiums. The company would then show a loss for writing the $100,000 in premiums until the premiums were earned.

The other method of reporting the financial condition of a stock company is the report to stockholders. This report contains information not included in the convention report, such as adjusted earnings and deferred taxes. The adjusted earnings in this report reflect expenses matched with income. This is called the going-concern method under generally accepted accounting principles. What happened here is that all of the expenses are absorbed as the premiums are earned over the course of the policy. A company writing $100,000 in premiums would show only that part of the expense generated as the premium is earned.

The report to stockholders is required of stock companies which are publicly traded, and a copy of this report must be submitted to the Securities and Exchange Commission annually.

An example of the two reporting methods is shown below. The company shown can be assumed to be a new company, and for the purposes of illustration the methods shown are not complete.

NOT ALWAYS A LOSS

Convention Report

Premiums written	$100,000
Less unearned premiums	90,000
Premiums earned	$ 10,000

Losses incurred	$ 5,000
Expenses incurred	40,000
Total losses and expenses	$ 45,000
Underwriting loss	$ 35,000

Stockholders' Annual Report/Adjusted Underwriting Results

Underwriting loss	$ 35,000
Increased equity in unearned premiums (35% of unearned premium)	31,500
Adjusted underwriting loss	$ 3,500
Net investment earnings	15,000
Total company profits	$ 11,500

It is understandable from the foregoing example, that stock insurers would hope to have their underwriting losses as contained in the convention report publicized; it is much more advantageous for the insurers to bemoan a loss of $35,000 than to mention a profit of $11,500. There is an exception to this, however, and that is in financial publications which would be read by the investing public. The stock insurers want their own stock to look attractive. They want investors to know that, despite poor underwriting years, they are still profitable enterprises.

Since 1950, insurance rates have increased 94 percent for bodily injury and property damage alone. Various consumer groups have been formed to protest these increases and have asked that investment income be considered in rate-making formulas. Several states have started to do this in recent years. Considering that some 50 percent of an insurer's invested funds have been provided by policyholders, this is the only fair way the problem can be resolved.

Almost every dollar paid to the insurers in the form of premiums represents investment income of either short-term or long-term duration. Significantly, even losses earn profits. When a claim is received, an estimate of the loss and the necessary expenses are transferred to the loss and loss-adjustment account. The longer the claim remains unpaid in this account, the longer assets are allowed to generate investment income. The larger the claim, the longer the waiting time before settlement. Some claims take as long as five years before settlement is made. The following simplified example illustrates the income generated by a $25,000 claim.

LOSSES MAKE PROFITS

Company estimate of claim loss	$25,000
15% loss adjustment expense	3,750
	$28,750
$28,750 invested for 5 years at 10% interest annually	$17,553
Total	$46,301
Paid to claimant at end of 5 years	$25,000
Profit on claim (minus loss-adjustment expense of $3,750)	$17,553

If investment income is to be considered in rate making, and it must, the suffering and hardship of thousands of claimants should not be used as an investment opportunity. Most of the insurers insist that the profits from the unearned premium reserve and the loss-adjustment reserves belong to them and not to the policyholders. Virginia is the only state that has legislated a definite and basically comprehensive profit formula. In 1965, that state ruled that the interest, dividends, and rents on the unearned premium reserves should be credited in the rate-making formula. Then, in 1969, the Virginia Insurance Commission reached its most recent conclusion:

> Investment income (interest, dividends, rents and realized capital gains) on the unearned premium and loss reserves would be considered, and the profit allowance fixed at 3.1 percent.

It is arguable whether states like New York, Kentucky, and New Hampshire, which include investment income in their rate making, have even scratched the surface in drafting effective legislation to control excessive profit making. To limit consideration of profits to the unearned premium and loss reserves is not sufficient. The entire investment portfolio should be considered. At least Virginia has gotten this far, but an even farther-reaching policy would be more desirable.

All of the states are concerned that the insurers within their states are operating on a sound financial basis. Too, it is in the best interests of the policyholders that this be so. The problem has been in determining what a fair and reasonable profit might be. There has been, perhaps, more written about the investments aspect of the insurers' business than any other. Formulas abound, contributed by government, the insurers, and the academic community, but no formula seems able to satisfy the question of a fair and reasonable profit. Consequently, there is no formula in general use across the country.

The American Insurance Association commissioned the research firm of Arthur D. Little, Inc., to investigate the profitability of stock insurers. ADL issued its report in November of 1967, and the high professional integrity of this firm would certainly indicate that no bias would be attached to their findings.

The report stated that there was no evidence of excessive profitability in the auto-insurance industry. The National Association of Insurance Commissioners and a host of professors from all over the country disputed some of the factors used in the analysis. Because these factors were in some cases fundamental, the results were not true, claimed the opponents of the report. Consequently, the issue is still unresolved.

An indication of the spread between different analyses is ADL's average of 7 percent return on net worth and a figure of 9.4 percent calculated by Mr. Dean Sharp, counsel for the Senate Antitrust and Monopoly Subcommittee. Mr. Sharp also indicated that the Allstate Group returned a profit of 20.9 percent on mean net worth after taxes. All of the Sharp figures have been contested, just as the Arthur D. Little figure has been. One other interesting point made in the Sharp report is that for the ten-year period 1959-1969, 13 of the largest auto insurance companies—including stock, mutual, and reciprocals—earned $788 million in underwriting profits, and they showed a net investment income of $3.26 billion. The lack of agreement among these authorities indicates the complete confusion existing within the insurance industry.

Regardless of the methods used in calculating profits, and regardless of who is right or wrong, it is evident that the insurers are making substantial profits. It is evident also that the policyholders are paying more. There are certain priorities that the entire insurance industry can agree to, however, and these are as follows:

The first and foremost factor in the stock insurance business is the policyholder. The second is the insurance company, and the third is the stockholder. The policyholder's needs, in the form of fair rates and good service, should come before anything else. The company, however, if it is to grow and offer stability, must make a profit. Also, the stockholders must receive some consideration for the use of their funds. The actual practice, of course, has been quite different.

It is apparently simple to pay lip service to priorities and to dismiss the policyholder from any other consideration than as a source of income. The profit pie has been so split that the stockholders receive anywhere from 25 percent up and the company the remainder. If the insurers had been true to their stated priorities, how could their rates have increased by some 60 percent in the 1957-1968 period, while the stockholders and the companies split up almost $5 billion in profits during the same period? How can any validity be given to the insurers' statements concerning their priorities and their lack of profitability in the face of these facts? Quite frequently the insurers will point to a single year as evidence of their unprofitability. This may be so. There are bad years in every business, but the good years more than make up for them. It is only across appreciable spans of time, ten years of more, that a fairly accurate picture of an insurer's profitability emerges. If the facts are allowed to speak for themselves, then the stock insurers have truly enjoyed many profitable nonprofit years.

MUTUALS AND PROFITABILITY

The largest automobile insurer in the country is State Farm Mutual Insurance Company. It has enjoyed this position since 1941. State Farm, despite its size, shares similar problems with all mutual auto insurers.

Because the mutuals are owned by the policyholders, and the nature of the relationship between the company and them prohibits the mutual from obtaining outside capital, all expansion needs must be generated from within. The paid-in premiums and investment income are the only significant sources of expansion funds.

The mutual insurer must also be financially prepared for any unanticipated heavy losses or unexpected expenditures. The company then must have a surplus over and above funds held for liabilities and other reserves. As the number of cars a company insures increases, so, too, must all surplus and reserve funds increase. The primary source of these funds is the policyholder.

The stock insurers and some of the mutuals have been remiss in recent years in not underwriting their share of the new car market. Estimates of 2.1 to 2.5 million cars are added to our national total of cars on the road each year.

Many of the old-line stock companies are content to sit back and not share in this responsibility. Too, some of the stock companies that have been taken over by the conglomerates and milked of their surplus cannot increase their underwriting capacity. This leaves the burden on State Farm, Nationwide, and Liberty, among the mutuals who have absorbed the bulk of the new cars. Allstate and Government Employees are the only two stock companies that have been responsive in this area.

At the request of the National Association of Insurance Commissioners, State Farm submitted a report of its surplus analysis, going back to the beginning of the company in 1922. The total underwriting and investment gain combined amounted to almost $617.5 million up to 1965. This gain has resulted in a surplus to policyholders of almost $471 million. In the NAIC evaluation of the report, the following excerpt is quoted:

> Sometimes the public is overcharged and exploited for the enrichment of others. Profits may be excessive. But

here, as the figures show, the "profit" is not being used to line someone's pocket; it is being used to satisfy a pressing public need ... more insurance capacity. Without the "profit" generated by State Farm over this period of years, the automobile insurance capacity problem might have become even more acute ....

In 1969, State Farm insured 11.5 million cars and incurred underwriting losses of $81.8 million. Investment income for the year amounted to $63.5 million. In addition, dividends of $10.2 million were paid, leaving a net loss to the company of $26.7 million, which in effect is a reduction in policyholders' surplus by that amount.

All mutuals are prohibited from forming upstream holding companies, and the restrictions placed on the investment portfolios are strictly regulated by the states. The consequences of these regulations is that the mutuals cannot take better advantage of the securities market. The stock companies are at least allowed to form holding companies, thereby circumventing investment restrictions. The mutuals do not enjoy this option. The future holds no promise that the mutuals will be able to operate under more liberal regulations, and their surplus requirements cannot be entirely met by the insured. Thus, the large mutuals face a possible slowdown and perhaps even a halt in their future growth.

STATE REGULATORY COMMISSIONS

The attitude of the general public toward regulatory agencies is one of indifference. Claims that they are in the pay of the industries they regulate are seldom wholly true. More often than not, the top echelon within the agencies are political appointees, more desirous of keeping their jobs, than of upsetting the status quo. Too, the job of regulation is often a complicated one and one that is rarely understood by the public. Richard E. Stewart, former New York Superintendent of Insurance, recently characterized the situation as follows:

> Left alone with each other, the regulator and his industry unconsciously find a mutual interest in ritualizing the relationship. The regulator must emphasize law and regularity, against the day he is challenged in court or denounced in public. He thus must look to form and detail, and may look away from the operating realities of the industry and from the expectations of the public. The industry relies on the ritual of regulation to make government behavior predictable, and to keep the regulator occupied in areas where interference can be tolerated. . . .

Up until more recent times, most of the states had insurance departments that were ritualized to a condition of impotence. Today, the majority of states are aware, at least, that the rituals have ended. In the remainder of the states ritual is still the substance of regulation, and in a few states even the ritual has been replaced with nothing but mere tokenism. A recent study of state insurance commissions indicates that the insurance laws of many states were inadequate, ambiguous, and obsolete. All of this implies a rather dreary regulatory situation.

Fortunately, in the last decade a new spirit has taken hold of state insurance departments. With a few exceptions, most of the states are trying desperately to bring their staffs up to efficient levels and to draft new legislation to strengthen the regulatory framework. Much of the credit for this new esprit must be given to the National Association of Insurance Commissioners. This organization is composed of the commissioners from each state, and in addition to many other benefits, it provides the commissioners with a forum to discuss new ideas. The NAIC is not a new organization, having been formed 100 years ago, but it has undergone a renaissance in recent years. The basic function of the NAIC is one of service to the states, which is accomplished through various standing committees and subcommittees. These committees function much like legislative bodies in that they hold hearings and recommend model legislation. Several of the standing committees provide services through securities evaluation and interstate examinations of insurers.

In order to understand what insurance regulation is, and how the automobile insurers are specifically regulated, we must look at the system in practice. The first priority of the regulator is to see that the insurer remains solvent. This also consists of assuring motorists that they will get the most insurance for their money. It means also that the rates charged by the insurers will not be excessive, inadequate, and unfairly discriminatory. Any motorist with a valid driver's permit should be able to obtain insurance coverage according to his needs and at reasonable prices. The insurer should abide by the provisions contained in an insurance policy without qualifications.

The second priority of the regulator is to be aware of the changing needs of the public and to adapt policy to these needs quickly and effectively. The third is to see that the insurers, as a group, are not unduly restrained in their efforts to operate as a reasonably profitable private enterprise.

Insurance policies are submitted to the state commissioners before they are offered to the motoring public. Commission attorneys evaluate the policies in terms of their conditions to see that they are complete and are not ambiguously worded. In states having prior-approval laws, rates are submitted by the insurers to the commission for evaluation. The commission will then allow or disallow rate changes according to specific criteria—such as rates that might be destructive of competition.

When a motorist purchases an insurance policy, he expects that the company insuring him is financially sound. The primary job of the regulatory department is to make sure that the insurance companies within the state live up to the trust of the public. The most costly function of the department is the company examining procedure.

Each company operating within a state must be examined every three years. A highly qualified examiner must go into an insurance company and audit the books; he must evaluate every detail of each financial transaction conducted by the company. For some large companies this procedure can take several months. A yearly check is made on each company through its convention reports. If an examiner is not satisfied with the financial condition of a company, he can recommend that it be suspended from further insurance operations until it can satisfy the objection, or he can recommend that the company be declared insolvent.

Many states have as many as 1,000 or more insurance companies operating in all lines of insurance. New York has over 300 examiners, while states like Alaska, Arizona, Mississippi, Oklahoma, and West Virginia, up until 1964, had none. Because mismanagement, illegal activities, and even depressed business conditions can cause a serious threat to the policyholder's interests, the regulator must be able to recognize the problem quickly. If examiners are not available to the regulator, insolvencies can occur, causing serious financial hardships to policyholders and claimants.

There are reasons for the attitudes of many insurance regulatory commissions which lie beyond the specter of ritual. Chief among these is inadequate funding. It does not make much sense to have an insurance department whose personnel are inferior to the insurers they regulate, nor does it make any sense to have the examiners paid by the insurance companies they are auditing. State insurance departments operate on an average of 4 percent of taxes and fees collected from the insurers. This amount is clearly not enough to finance effective regulatory departments. A 1964 study showed that Illinois's commission operated on a budget of $1.3 million, or 3.64 percent of total taxes and fees. This is one reason, perhaps, why Illinois has had one of the poorest records of insurance insolvencies in the country. The state had only 47 examiners for 1,281 companies in that year.

Every state insurance department must have personnel who are well paid and who are at least the equal in technical skills of the insurance companies they regulate. New York is noted as having the finest insurance department in the country, both in terms of personnel and regulatory excellence. The most recent figures available indicate that the department's budget for 1969 was $8.7 million. The total revenue received by the state in taxes and fees from the insurers was $118.8 million. Therefore, the New York department was funded at a level of 6.1 percent.

It must be noted also that other states may not have tax laws allowing for substantial tax revenues to be collected from the insurers. Quite often, too, the allocation of tax revenues by the states is not based upon any income an agency might generate. Every state is hard pressed to finance the needs of its citizens, but the deprivation and hardship caused by an insolvent insurer makes it mandatory that the insurance regulatory agency be funded above political considerations.

The insurers have their responsibilities to the regulators as well as to policyholders. Basically, what this amounts to is the insurers' attitudes toward change. The insurer must

41

be aware of changing social needs and be able to adapt to these needs. Many insurers today are not only finding it difficult to see that change is needed, but to institute new programs when they finally recognize the problem.

Many of the old-line insurance companies do not realize that change can be productive. These insurers are spending millions of dollars to preserve the practices of the past because they cannot or will not face the realities of today. Instead of treating change as a constructive force, these insurers look upon it as a destructive evil. This resistance to change only serves to make the progressive regulator's job more difficult, and occasionally impossible. The one caveat that all must recognize, however, is that change for the sake of change is unnecessary and destructive. Change that is responsive to today's needs, and that will serve the social needs of the foreseeable future, is absolutely necessary.

POLITICS
AND THE STATE COMMISSIONS

Many of the reasons for the problems of state insurance departments center around the state legislatures, but the problem has its roots in the cities and towns of each state. The rituals that have evolved between the regulators and the insurers require that the regulators stay within certain bounds of effectiveness. To go beyond these bounds, it is important that a well-qualified and well-paid commissioner be hired who, in turn, will staff his department with personnel who are willing to forgo the rituals for operational efficiency. A move of this sort can only be accomplished through a state governor who owes nothing to the insurance companies.

The governor can play his politics in getting his man appointed as commissioner. The difficulty here, as in the case of obtaining more funds for the insurance department, is with the legislators controlled by the insurers. The tentacles of the insurance establishment reach into every town and city in the country, through the offices of insurance agents and brokers. These men who work directly for the insurer, or indirectly as independent brokers, are usually local men. They are respected members of the community in which they work and are very active in civic affairs. These men also expend much effort and spend much money to assist politicians in their bids for reelection, in return for favoring the interests of the insurers. These men will also back the political tyro who makes it known that he will be friendly toward the insurance industry.

Attorneys are another factor in the control of the legislatures. The legal profession is well represented in the ranks of the legislators. On the average, trial lawyers receive some 50 percent of their incomes from automobile-accident cases. In their own interests they will work to defeat any bill that threatens their livelihood. The recent debacle in Massachusetts over no-fault auto insurance is a good example of the power of these attorneys, working in concert with the insurers to produce a no-fault law that is, at best, a poor relief for the public. It took over four years of constant fighting, of concessions, and of arbitration to produce an almost worthless bill.

A liberated insurance commissioner recently characterized the workings of state legislatures as follows:

> The workings of the legislative process are indeed strange and wonderful to behold. No circumstance renders this more apparent than the life-or-death struggle over the fate of a controversial bill. In such a struggle

no holds are barred, and the legislators are regarded as pawns in the hands of expert players, to be manipulated according to the skill of the mover.

It is sad to think of our legislators as being mere pawns in a giant chess game, but that is what they seem to be. They are virtually in the employ of the various insurance lobbies that plague the halls of government. Those few who are the honest and dedicated champions of the public interest are too seldom heard.

The issue of state control versus federal control of insurers is before us. The ability of the states to respond to the needs of a growing and dynamic society will be shown in the next two years. If the states cannot regulate the auto insurers to the satisfaction of the motoring public, then the federal government will have to take over. We will then have federal control of the insurance industry, or we will have federal auto insurance similar in administration to that of the Social Security Administration.

INSOLVENCIES

Mary Louise Simpson was 53 years old on her last birthday. She has no family and works as an assembler in a factory earning $205 per month take-home pay. Her greatest luxury is a 1955 Ford sedan which she bought in 1967. When Mary purchased her car, she went to a local broker and asked to buy automobile insurance. She had never owned a car before and knew nothing about insurance. The insurance broker took down all the particulars, and Mary signed a contract. She paid the broker $463 for the basic coverage of bodily injury and property damage. As far as Mary was concerned, the broker *was* the insurance company. He determined that, because of the neighborhood she lived in and her age, she would not qualify for any of the major insurance companies. He placed her with a small company that specialized in high-risk insurance. The company was an assessable mutual, and they were paying high commission rates. He forwarded Mary's application and forgot about her.

One day Mary received a notice in the mail that her insurer had been declared insolvent, and that she had 30 days in which to purchase insurance from another company. Just the month before, she had paid her 1968 premium in full out of her savings. Mary called her insurance broker for advice. The broker told her that he had received other telephone calls complaining of the same problem; all he could offer was to find another insurer for Mary. She then had to pay another $463 for a new policy. Mary had no choice, because her car was necessary to travel to the factory. She closed out her savings account and purchased another policy from the broker. This time she implored the broker to place her with a company that would not become insolvent. Fortunately, he was to place her with a high-risk insurer, which was a subsidiary of one of the large national companies. (There have been cases where a policyholder lost his insurance because of an insolvent company and who purchased another policy only to have the second insurer become insolvent as well. The State of Illinois has been particularly hazardous for the auto-insurance policyholder in this regard.)

Two months later Mary received another notice, this time informing her that she had to pay $320 as an assessment to the receivers of the insolvent company she had been insured with. Mary went to her local legal-aid society and explained her problem. There she was advised to pay the additional money and told that the law was very explicit in her case. She had purchased insurance from an assessable mutual and contained within her auto policy was a provision of contingent liability. This means that she, as part owner of the insurance company, was obligated to pay for the company's losses up to the assessable limits as stated in her policy. Mary was able to borrow enough money to pay the assessment, but it is doubtful that she ever understood what happened to her.

There is another aspect of the insolvency problem that has far more severe repercussions. Peter Robison was involved in a serious accident in which he was clearly at fault. He unthinkingly ran a red light on his way to work, colliding with another vehicle and seriously injuring its three occupants. The case eventually came to trial, and damages of $18,000 were awarded the plaintiffs. Unfortunately, Peter's insurer had been declared insolvent some time before. The receivers of the company decreed that $3,000 was all of the money that was available for Peter from the insolvent insurer's assets. Peter was liable, therefore, for the remaining $15,000 plus his own attorney's fees.

Peter, his wife, and four children were forced to sell their home and move into a low-rent apartment. The proceeds from the sale of the house after taxes amounted to $6,000. The balance of $9,000 will be paid in monthly installments for the next six years. In addition, Peter was liable for another $190 for an assessment from his insolvent insurer.

These cases are absurd. While the policyholders purchased what they thought was a policy of insurance to protect them from financial loss, in effect, they purchased financial disaster.

A profile of an insolvent insurer is usually that of a high-risk assessable mutual. The reasons for this are many. An insurer can set up shop with as little as $200,000 and be on its way. Boxford General Casualty Mutual Insurance

Company* was one of these. In just three years, the company's principals got away with over $5 million. The money was used to decorate plush offices, extensive gardening at the home of the principals, vacations, and outside investments. Expensive call girls were installed in lush apartments for the use of certain business acquaintances. All of these things were done over a period of three years, and never once were they discovered. Or, perhaps, it might be better to say that no one reported them. State examiners were thrown off the track by the use of false securities and careful falsification of records. A subsidiary company in another state was used to assist them in their securities swaps. Finally, the raft of complaints received by the state insurance department from claimants prompted a complete investigation. The findings by the state revealed mismanagement and fraud, which led to the subsequent declaration of insolvency. The principals were brought to trial in federal court on charges of interstate fraud. Other state charges are pending. This is not the only occurrence of mismanagement and outright thievery; there have been many more. Unfortunately, many of these criminals receive a mere slap on the wrist from the courts and are freed to set up the same kinds of illegal operations in other states. The State of Illinois characterizes punishment for wealthy criminals as follows:

> There is little punishment deterrent for wrongdoing with the entire legal process, basic laws relating to financial crime, rules of evidence, legal processing, delays and appeals, all favoring the wealthy criminal who can employ expensive, technically skilled lawyers paid to defend clients and not to further social causes,

---

*The name of this company and other details have been changed due to litigation proceedings still under way.

this minimizing the chances of indictment, trial and conviction and the actual serving of a prison term. . . .

State laws are remiss in allowing mutual insurers to begin operations with low surplus requirements ($200,000). The states are even more at fault for not keeping these companies under the closest possible scrutiny until their managements prove they can operate honestly and efficiently.

In the Commonwealth of Pennsylvania, files of the insurance department indicate that 33 property and liability insurers became insolvent, or were suspended, during the last 30 years. Each of these companies was issuing at least one type of automobile insurance coverage. Of the total, 31 companies were mutuals and two were stock companies. Thirty of the mutuals were issuing limited assessment policies at the time of liquidation. The greater majority of these companies were issuing high-risk policies as well. Between 1960 and 1968, 17 companies were declared insolvent with an average assessment of $120 for each of the 210,000 policyholders. On a 25-state basis, for the same period, 652,939 policyholders were assessed over $69 million. In addition, the loss to claimants is estimated at over $100 million.

For the layman unschooled in the intricacies of financial analysis, the insurance industry is a formidable jungle of figures and legal terminology. The only contact most people have with an insurance company is with an agent or broker. These men would not ordinarily have the qualifications to pass on the financial health of any company they worked for, nor would any of them want to assume that sort of responsibility. Their primary purpose is that of middlemen, whose interest in the insured is confined to the commissions they receive for placing their insurance. Under the best regulatory supervision insolvencies will occur. The New York Insurance Department has a task force working on the problem, and it is expected that they will make recommendations for even stricter laws than the state already possesses.

Because of the near impossibility of completely resolving the insolvency problem, another method of protection for the motorist has had to be devised. In 1939, New York passed the first insolvency-protection fund, and in 1947 a bill with even broader protection for motorists and pedestrians was passed. This bill created what is known as the Motor Vehicle Liability Fund, and provided that the fund would assume the claims-payment responsibilities of insolvent insurers. Other states have followed suit, and it is hoped that funds of this kind will be in operation in every state soon.

THE GREED OF THE
CONGLOMERATES

In 1968 the conglomerates invaded the insurance industry, and at the end of that year, $4.1 billion of the industry's assets were controlled by the invaders. These take-overs raise some serious questions, in view of their subsequent effect on the insurance industry. Many of the old-line stock companies have accumulated vast surpluses over the years, and these surpluses represent valuable prizes to the cash-hungry conglomerates. As we shall see, one of the first moves by the acquiring conglomerate is to give itself a bonus out of the surplus in the form of a dividend. The effect of this upon the insurer is to weaken its financial strength so that it is not able to take up the ever-increasing demands for an expanding auto-insurance market and to reduce its capacity to withstand catastrophes, like Hurricane Camille, which do occur regularly. The managements of the conglomerates are not versed in the insurance business. All these companies want is to milk the insurers

49

in order to finance further acquisitions. The overreaching of these corporate Goliaths eventually catches up with them, as in the case of Ling-Tempco-Vought, which found itself in serious financial trouble in 1970, and had to divest itself of some of its holdings.

During the midsixties, the conglomerates were the darlings of Wall Street; their stocks were selling at between 40 and 60 times earnings. The insurers, however, who historically have seen their stocks undervalued in periods of high inflation, were easy prey for the conglomerates, because their price-earnings ratios were often below book value. This meant that the conglomerates could make tender offers to the stockholders of the insurers, which if accepted, would cost the conglomerates little or no cash due to the price differential. A market broker's analysis of a company's stock would illustrate: conglomerate A's stock is selling at 50 times earnings of 85 cents or $42.50; insurer B's stock is selling at 12 times earnings of 85 cents, or $10.20. The conglomerate could afford to offer one share of its stock for three shares of the insurer's stock. This would allow an immediate profit to the shareholder of the insurer stock of $9.35 after consideration for dividends. When this profit is added to the possibility of even further appreciation in the conglomerate's stock, the offer is hard to refuse. Of course, these are all paper profits, and the dependability of insurer dividends is far greater than that of the high-flying conglomerates. The method illustrated above is only one used by the conglomerates, and it is simplified. Interestingly enough, when the market turned around in 1969 and then plummeted in 1970, the paper profits and expected dividends of the conglomerates never materialized. Other methods used in the take-overs involved a combination of securities offered to shareholders of the insurance companies. Known as "funny money," these combinations were comprised of stock warrants, preferred stock, and debentures.

Several conglomerate take-overs were exceptional at the time they occurred, and the acquisition of Great American Holding Company by National General was one of the most spectacular.

In November of 1968, National General, a holding company with interests in numerous business fields such as motion pictures, banking, and publishing, acquired Great American Holding Company, parent of Great American Insurance Company. National General, with assets of only $48 million in 1967, was able to acquire Great American which had assets of $600 million. The offer made to the shareholders of Great American consisted of an exchange of $50 principal amount, 4 percent convertible debentures, convertible at $48.50 per share, plus warrants of 1.5 shares of National's stock at $40 per share. This "funny money" package amounted to an indebtedness of $500 million by National General, or in more simple terms National General borrowed $500 million based on assets of $48 million to purchase a company worth $600 million. National's first act was to declare a special dividend to its shareholders of approximately $174 million from the surplus of Great American Insurance Company. Since National owned 97 percent of Great American's outstanding stock, National in effect paid itself three times its actual worth as a bonus.

During the height of the trading activity between National and Great American, both stocks reached impressive peaks. The high for National's stock was $56.25, reached in the last quarter of 1968. Great American reached a high of $86 during the same period. The low for National in 1970 was a pitiful $9 per share, while in January of 1971 National did climb to $21.25. There are, of course, no figures for Great American for 1970 as yet, but historically, insurance stocks have weathered recessions and depressions far better than most stocks. Great American shareholders who traded their stock for National's must have been dismayed to see all of National's prospect in capital gains slide into a capital loss.

National General's acquisition of Great American enabled National to get into the big time. But one thing National did not take into account was the watchful eye of the New York Insurance Department. Great American Insurance Company was found to have violated the Holding Company Law of 1969 and other insurance laws in the fall of 1970. In addition to alleged illegal trading of stocks in Great American's portfolio and other investment violations, various officers and members of the board of directors of Great American were charged with being pecuniarily interested in the acquisition of Armour and Company by General Host Corporation. On or about February 7, 1969, it was charged, Great American purchased 324,900 shares of Armour's common stock at a cost of $23,180,103.69. Then on February 23, 1969, Great American exchanged its Armour stock for $17,494,000 in General Host 7 percent subordinated debentures and 812,250 warrants to purchase General Host common at $40 per share. Most of the members of Great American's board of directors are also on the board of National General.

Accordingly, on December 3, 1970, the largest fine ever imposed by the New York Insurance Department was levied against Great American for $100,000 and another fine of $500 against Constellation Reinsurance Corporation, a subsidiary of Great American. These fines were paid without any admission of guilt.

Most companies play games on the stock market with their own securities and the securities of others, and if the Securities and Exchange Commission cannot control it, that is one thing. Playing games with insurance-company investment portfolios is another matter; funds belonging to innocent policyholders and accident victims are not a commodity to be traded in the marketplace.

Another brow-raising take-over was that of Reliance Insurance Company, with assets of $750 million, by Leasco Data Processing Equipment Corporation, with assets of $74.2 million. Leasco gained control in September, 1968, eventually acquiring 97 percent of Reliance's stock.

The rape of Reliance began almost immediately, with a dividend of $7 declared by Reliance, amounting to $38 million in the coffers of Leasco. On September 28, 1969, Leasco announced that it had borrowed $40 million for a period of two years, using 62 percent of their Reliance stock as security. Leasco's "funny money" offer consisted of $72 in its preferred and warrants for each Reliance share. Leasco made further guarantees to certain stockholders that the $72 package would be pledged through deals with a number of other insurance companies and banks. In return, Leasco promised the lenders that they would receive $600,000 a month in interest for every month the stock was held. This amounted to an interest rate of 12.5 percent.

For the remaining Reliance stockholders who bought the Leasco package, and who did not sell it in late '68 or early '69, the deal turned out to be far less profitable. In July of 1970 the package was worth approximately $27, down 63 percent since the merger. The Securities and Exchange Commission might well ponder the fairness of guaranteed sales for certain large investors, while small stockholders with no such guarantees took their lumps.

In all, there were 13 major insurance-company acquisitions by the conglomerates in 1968. The pace has slowed considerably, because of tight money markets and depressed stock-market conditions.

To the casual observer, the activities of the conglomerates and the insurance companies is meaningless; to him the world of corporate infighting is strange. But, as we have pointed out, the effects of these take-overs can hurt the motoring public. Every acquisition by a noninsurance company of an insurer carries with it the potential for surplus dilution and other dangers. Only those state insurance departments with highly trained experts will be able to cope with the financial wizardry of the corporate raiders. Anything less than that will lead to disastrous consequences for the insured.

INSURANCE HOLDING COMPANIES

The major difference between a holding company and a conglomerate is that the holding company is simply a corporate device used for financial purposes. The conglomerate, on the other hand, is centered around a company that manufactures some product or sells some service.

In most states there are no limitations as to the kinds of companies a holding company may acquire. The federal government restricts acquisitions if they fall under the provisions of the Sherman Antitrust Laws or other laws.

Insurance holding companies can be formed in either of two ways. The first form of holding company is where an insurer elects to form a holding company that will control the stock of the parent company. This is known as an upstream holding company. The second form is the downstream holding company. In this case, a subsidiary of the insurer forms a holding company with the parent insurer owning the stock of the subsidiary and hence the holding company. Each of these forms is used as circumstance allows or dictates.

The reasons for the formation of a holding company by an insurer are many. Because of strict regulatory laws restricting investments within certain prescribed limits, insurers found that the holding-company device would allow them the freedom to invest some surplus funds as they chose. The holding-company device allowed them to extend some insurance lines and to acquire others. In addition, there are certain tax benefits and borrowing powers the holding company enjoys that a nonholding company cannot use. For many years these holding companies have been formed within the insurance industry. For as long as these holding companies restricted themselves to acquiring companies that were at least related to insurance, state insurance departments were not overly concerned. In the last decade, however, insurance holding companies have gradually drifted into many unrelated businesses.

New York's former superintendent of insurance, Richard E. Stewart, recognized the problem shortly after taking office in 1967 and commissioned a blue-ribbon panel of experts to make a complete evaluation of the holding companies. In 1968, the group published its findings, entitled *Report of the Special Committee on Insurance Holding Companies.*

Included in the report were specific recommendations to minimize the need of insurance companies to form holding companies and measures to control any acquisitions of a holding company or conglomerate. In part the summary of the report said:

> We have concluded that the holding company device, when it involves affiliation with non-insurance enterprises, jeopardizes the interest of both the public and the policyholder, and especially will do so if its development is indiscriminate and without benefit of close regulatory supervision.

Many of the recommendations contained in the report were drafted into legislation and became law in 1969. Thus

New York became the first state in the country to establish effective control over acquisitions which were not in the best interests of the public. The National Association of Insurance Commissioners had drafted model legislation prior to the New York report, which is under study in many states for controlling acquisitions.

During the years 1960-1968, there were 580 acquisitions and mergers of property and liability insurance companies involving $10 billion in admitted assets. Concentration of power within the insurance companies was growing. In 1969, the top 20 insurers sold approximately 50 percent of all auto insurance sold. If this practice were allowed to continue, the insurers would dwindle to a mere few and would destroy the competitiveness that is essential to a healthy insurance industry.

The insurance companies were unprepared for the rash of acquisitions by the holding companies and the conglomerates. For many years they had been content to build their surpluses through restrictive underwriting practices and through substantial investment profits. The attitudes of the insurers in the late fifties is no better stated than in the following speech of Shelby Cullom Davis, former New York insurance stock specialist and the present ambassador to Switzerland. At the Eighth Hemispheric Insurance Conference in Lima, Peru, in October of 1961, he said in part:

> In general, if a company's capital and surplus is over 100 per cent of its unearned premium, it is considered to be in a comfortable underwriting position as far as capacity is concerned. Of the 68 companies which we survey annually, 19 were in this position, capital and surplus were 100 per cent or more of unearned premiums. In this group are such well-known groups as Federal, Continental Insurance, Phoenix, Insurance Company of North America, Great American, United

States Fire, Home, and St. Paul Fire and Marine. . . . I suppose every company would like to be in the top category, the least exposed or conversely the group having the most underwriting capacity. *Certainly it is the most enviable position.* *

There have been changes in the industry in the last ten years. Of the so-called enviable group mentioned in this speech, each has undergone some form of corporate change.

Company	Acquired by:
Federal Insurance	Chubb & Sons, Inc.
Continental Insurance	Continental Corporation
Phoenix Insurance	Travelers Corporation
Insurance Company of North America	INA Corporation
Great American Insurance	National General
United States Fire	Crumm & Forster
Home Insurance Company	City Investing
St. Paul Fire and Marine	The St. Paul Companies, Inc.

The foregoing can only illustrate the apparent naïveté of the insurers in the early sixties. Some of these corporate changes were prompted through fear of the conglomerate raiders. More were prompted by the desire to escape the yoke of the state insurance departments and their investment restrictions. In any event, the halcyon days of the insurance companies are over. It can be imagined that all of these companies are keeping a watchful eye on the corporate giants around them.

A total of 174 new automobile-insurance companies were formed in the 1955-1968 period. Existing insurance companies were responsible for the formation of 66 of

---

* Emphasis supplied.

companies, leaving the remaining 108 companies
..ri no prior affiliation. During the last several years, however, the number of new entrants into the automobile-
insurance business has decreased appreciably. The new
entrants at least were contributing a small part of the over-
all capacity that has been lost through the greed of the
conglomerates and some of the holding companies. Now
with new entries decreasing, the capacity of the entire industry to meet its obligations to the growing motoring
public is even more weakened. Hopefully, the states will
follow New York's lead and sharply reduce further diminu-
tion of insurance resources.

RATES AND RATE MAKING

All men are equal in the eyes of God, and some are more
equal than others, but in the eyes of the automobile-
insurance companies all men are risks and therefore un-
equal. The business of insurance today is the selection of
those risks that are unlikely to be involved in auto accidents. The insurers will go to any lengths to uncover these
prize drivers, for they are the darlings of the insurers—the
guaranteed, profit-making sweethearts of the risk-
calculated world. The enemies are those who just *might* be
in accidents. These are the pariahs—the tainted thieves who
will rob the insurers of their profits, dividends, and next
year's bonuses.

At one time, purchasing auto insurance was a simple
matter. One merely gave his name, address, and make of
car, paid his premium, and he was insured. It made no
difference whether the applicant was 17 or 75, man or
woman, the premium for all applicants was the same.
Through the years, many changes have taken place. Today,
the situation is approaching the absurd. There is virtually a

58

different rate for every motorist. However, the process of rarefied selection is not complete, and it will not be complete until the insurers have every objective and subjective human characteristic classified. The objective classifications are somewhat logical in that they apply to a person's age, marital status, occupation, and the like, but the subiective classifications are something else. The analysis ·of the behavioral characteristics of applicants adds unimaginable possibilities of new classifications. The insurers are going so far that even the inclusion of Gregor Mendel's three laws of genetics will probably play an important role in type classifications as well. To take this absurdity even further, it can be imagined that some day the insurers will be able to classify a person before he is born. (A blue-eyed male bred to a hazel-eyed female can only produce a brown-eyed, accident-prone baby.) The following are a partial list of subjective factors used in risk selection:

Driver's home environment: Clean house? Dirty house?
Driver's associates: Rowdy? Drinkers?
Moral character: Drinks? Chases women? Visits mother regularly?
Financial reputation: Always in debt? Sometimes?
Cooperation: Resents authority? Too individualistic?
Job stability: More than one job in two years?

This type of information is procured through the use of specialized investigative services, paid for by the insurers, and virtually every new applicant is investigated by them. The investigator will visit the applicant's neighborhood and talk with neighbors, storekeepers, tavern owners, and anyone else who might shed some light on the applicant's character. They will utilize retail credit reports, police reports, motor-vehicle department reports, and any other source available to further their investigation. The prob-

59

lems that this sort of investigation leads to are numerous. Your neighbor, angry that you chased his dog two years ago, can ruin you. He might tell them that the party you had last month was an uproarious, drunken melee, when actually it was a quiet cocktail party that ended at 8 P.M. There have been many cases of this sort and undoubtedly there will be many more. One case history of a nonrenewal by an auto insurer began with a notice of nonrenewal, then the following letter.

February 19, 1969

Mrs. Troy:

In answer to your letter of February 11, 1969, the reason your policy is not being renewed is because of unfavorable information we have received concerning personal habits within your household.

XYZ Insurance Company

Mrs. Troy, 26, was married to a retired marine sergeant, and they lived in Monroe, Virginia. The notice of non-renewal had come as a surprise to the Troys. Mr. Troy had had a minor accident that was paid for under his comprehensive coverage. In addition, he had received a traffic ticket for speeding several years before. The Troys were infuriated with the answer they received from the insurer giving as a reason for nonrenewal that there was something wrong with their personal habits. The Commonwealth of Virginia requires that the specific reason for insurance cancellation be given by the insurer, and the insurer's reason was certainly not specific. After much letter writing to the authorities in Virginia and Washington, Senator Hart, chairman of a subcommittee looking into the auto-insurance industry, became interested in the case. The Senator's staff investigated the situation, which resulted in subpoenas for the insurance company, the agent that sold the Troys insurance, the retail credit company hired by the insurer, and the Troys to appear before the subcommittee.

The resulting testimony showed that the investigator for the insurer had secured statements from only two merchants in Monroe and only one of these had made a derogatory statement concerning Mr. Troy. The merchant allowed that Mr. Troy was a heavy drinker and that he got drunk in his home frequently. The other merchant stated that he was puzzled as to why a young girl like Mrs. Troy would have married a man so much older than herself.

Further investigation by the Senator's staff revealed that the merchant making the allegation concerning Mr. Troy's drinking habits had never been in the Troy house. In fact, the merchant made a notarized statement to the subcommittee that he had never seen Mr. Troy drink more than three beers, that he had never seen Mr. Troy intoxicated, and that as far as he was concerned the gentleman was of good character. Statements were obtained from several more merchants, the sheriff's office, and the local justice of the peace. All of these statements were to the effect that the Troys were fine people of good character. Mr. Troy's service record indicated that he had had an excellent career as a marine with decorations, letters of commendation, and that he had never had a single court-martial in his entire 20 years in the Corps.

The final analysis of the case showed that the investigator had probably taken Mr. Troy's three beers and blown it up to where the man was accused of being a loud and boisterous drunk. The facts proved conclusively that Mr. Troy was a man of normal habits and a man with an excellent character. Virginia levied a fine of $500 against the insurer for failing to give proper notice of their reasons for nonrenewal.

The Troys were subjected to undue harassment for no good cause, because of what appears to be the incompetence of an investigator who cared only to report his quota of derogatory information. A letter to the editor printed in the *Wall Street Journal* of February 10, 1968, indicates how important this quota is:

> In your excellent article "Prying for Pay" in your February 5, 1968, issue, your investigators failed to let the cat out of the bag. The cat in question is the fact that I, or any insurance investigator employed by the largest firms in the business are required to turn in at least 15 per cent "protective information" on risks. "Protective" is really derogatory. An inspector who does not meet this quota quickly loses his job. It thus logically follows that the eager beaver quickly learns to make the 15 per cent or more, whether through earnest reporting or fabrication. Here is the serious flaw in the whole investigative business. The insurance companies rate their investigation firms by the percentage of "protective" information furnished. So the companies compete with each other to dig up as much "dirt" as possible, real or fancied. . . .

As we stated earlier, risk selection is the business of insurance, but prying into the lives of the insured with the services of incompetent investigators is not and should not be necessary or allowed. It is, in fact, an invasion of privacy, and legislation should be enacted to put a stop to this practice.

Perhaps the most unusual case of cancellation to come to light is that of a man in Missouri who had purchased over $100,000 worth of insurance for his auto and farm equipment. A month later he received a notice of cancellation. In reply to his letter requesting a reason for the cancellation, the insurer replied:

> We understand you have filed a damage suit against a carnival because it operated gambling games at the

county fair in your county (Douglas County, Mo.), and we believe you have so angered the citizens in your area, that if you were involved in an accident, even if not at fault, a local jury would find against you.

This sort of case makes one wonder about the difficulty a representative of the Internal Revenue Service might face in obtaining insurance.

For many years the process of rate making has been regarded as a science by the insurers. This development of rating systems which systematically subdivide a population of motorists is rationalized on the grounds that insurance prices should most closely approximate a driver's loss potential. Rating establishes many different groups with varying loss potentials. When competitive underwriting is allowed to dominate the rating structure, the more selective the group becomes. It is known that in any rating group only a small number of the insured will actually have accidents. Competition forces the insurer to rarefy its selection process further to screen out the undesirables and thereby offer lower rates. The insurer who is able to accomplish this can show substantial profits. The continuing process of screening creates a vast market of motorists who have been *refused* insurance and who must apply to other markets for coverage.

Drivers who are rejected do not necessarily have to be bad drivers, but they will be drivers whose rating characteristics cause them to be placed in a group where their qualifications do not meet the standards of the group. The applicant then must either find a standard insurer whose rating classes allow for his characteristics, or he must apply to the assigned-risk market.

As we stated earlier, the process of risk selection subdivides the motoring population into groups. The Insurance Rating Board has the so-called 260 class plan, and

63

it is currently in use by some 40 to 50 percent of the insurers. The plan contains 52 classifications, making distinctions by age, sex, marital status, and driver training, which is further augmented by five types of use classifications. A secondary classification is based upon the driver's accident experience and traffic violations. Under the Safe Driver Plan, those with clean records are allowed a discount of 17 percent. For those who have had accidents and traffic violations the surcharge rate is from 30 to 180 percent. The final determination under the IRB 260 class plan is the territorial variation schedule. The territories range from one in the District of Columbia to more than 60 in the State of New York. Motorists in rural areas pay less than those in urban areas with many variations in between the two extremes.

The actual rates under the 260 plan used by IRB companies is arrived at by multiplying the sum of the primary and secondary rating factors by the territorial base rate. To illustrate rate determinations under the plan, we start with a base territorial rate of $127. This is for $50,000 and $100,000 limits in the Los Angeles central area. If we suppose the applicant were a youthful, unmarried male, we could safely assume that he would pay between $127 and $711 depending on his primary and secondary rating factors. In other states the cost could be as high as $1,500. When all discounts and surcharges are taken into account, there are a total of 4,800 possible rates for each territory. For the State of Rhode Island, with three territories, this would mean a possible 14,400 rates. In New York, with 60 territories, it would mean 288,000 rate groupings.

We can see here that the addition of subjective factors to the 260 class plan would mean an incalculable number of rate variations.

The remaining insurers which do not subscribe to the IRB 260 class plan are the direct writers like Allstate and

State Farm, among the larger writers. Most of the smaller companies subscribe to the plan, but there are a few that do not. Erie Insurance Exchange of Erie, Pennsylvania, has been underwriting automobile insurance policies for over 40 years. In 1926 they had just one rate, now they have four. Erie has never had an underwriting loss and has never failed to pay a dividend of between 10 and 30 percent of premium each year.

In general, the present rating system, with its emphasis on even greater selectivity, is serving to force more drivers to underinsure or not to insure at all. In addition, despite these elaborate rating schemes, there are many insurers who will not provide coverage for certain risks. These motorists are presently looking to the assigned-risk plans for coverage.

THE ASSIGNED RISK MARKET

The insurers have created a limbo called the assigned-risk market for their rejects. It is the last stop before the hell of the high-risk market and home for more than 3 million motorists. Approximately 37 percent of the assigned-risk population is made up of people in low-paying occupations. The semiskilled, unskilled, agricultural workers, hotel and restaurant workers, and the unemployed are all forced into this expensive, inferior facility for several reasons: because they do not live in white, middle-class neighborhoods, because they are black or Puerto Rican, and for reasons of accidents, motor-vehicle violations, and lack of driving experience. The people who can least afford it are forced to pay higher auto-insurance premiums, a situation over which they have little control.

We recognize that the process of risk selection is one of discrimination, but it should be selection based mainly upon driving abilities and certain other objective criteria. The blatant racial, environmental, and occupational discrimination practiced by the insurers is abhorrent to the best interests of a civilized society.

The first assigned-risk plan went into effect in New Hampshire on May 10, 1938. Since that time, every state has adopted some form of an assigned-risk facility. Assigned-risk plans are most often voluntary organizations of insurers within the states. In each state there is a plan manager who receives applications and then assigns the applicants to various companies within the state according to quotas set by the governing board of the plan. The applicants are assigned according to the volume of business each insurer does within the state. For example, an insurer that had a volume of $20 million a year would be obliged to accept four or five times the number of applicants as the insurer doing $5 million a year. There are some changes taking place within the industry as to the administration of the plans. It has been found that regional centers which serve the needs of several states allow for administrative savings, and it is anticipated that there will be four such regions set up in the near future.

A motorist must first apply to the voluntary insurance market and be refused before application can be made to the assigned-risk market. Even here only certain risks are acceptable. The Illinois provisions for acceptability are typical:

Section 9, Eligibility

... A risk shall not be entitled to insurance nor shall any subscriber be required to afford or continue insurance under the following circumstances:

(A) If the applicant and/or anyone who normally or usually drives the automobile or anyone who drives it with the knowledge of the applicant is engaged in an illegal enterprise, or has been convicted of any felony during the immediately preceding three years or habitually disregards local or state laws as evidenced by two or more non-motor vehicle convictions during the immediate preceding three years.

(B) When during the immediately preceding three years the applicant and/or anyone who usually drives the automobile has suffered more than once the suspension or revocation of his operator's license or operating privilege or has been convicted or forfeited bail as follows. . . .

The Illinois plan goes on to list offenses such as driving under the influence of intoxicating liquors or narcotics, speeding, reckless driving, permitting an unlicensed person to drive, and so on for a total of 12 offenses. The Illinois plan also eliminates coverage if

1. The automobile insurance premiums are not paid;

2. The automobile is in a dangerous state of repair;

3. One who normally drives the automobile has a major mental or physical disability (total deafness, total blindness, epilepsy, double amputee of arms and/or legs;

4. Anyone who drives the automobile does not have a valid driver's license, except where the license has been suspended or revoked and can be restored upon filing proof of financial responsibility.

The most common method of obtaining coverage under the assigned-risk plan is to submit an application through an agent or broker. These representatives of the insurers are seldom willing to process applications, because their commission rates are considerably lower than for normal policy applications. The applications must be accompanied by a deposit of $25 in Colorado, $35 in Illinois, and $75 in California. Other states, such as New Jersey and Pennsylvania, require a deposit of 30 percent of premium. Eleven states currently require the full annual premium with the application. These states are Georgia, Massachusetts, Virginia, Vermont, Texas, Tennessee, South Carolina, Ohio, New Hampshire, and Maine. In addition, fees are collected in some states for processing applications.

A common effective date for coverage is two working days following the date of the application. Forty states issue policies within this time period. The remaining states may take from three to 15 days for approval. When the insurance company binds an applicant, payment for the balance of the premium is due within 15 to 30 days. If the applicant should be found unacceptable by the insurer to which his application has been assigned by the plan facility, the binder is canceled, and the premium returned. The applicant is then forced into the high-risk market. A complete description of this market follows this section on assigned risks.

The appointed carrier usually assumes the risk for a period of three years. Each year the insured is notified that his insurance will or will not be renewed. If the applicant performs satisfactorily in the assigned-risk market for his three years, he is then allowed to apply for insurance in the voluntary market. Most states provide coverage in the assigned-risk plan at limits of $10,000 for injury to one person and $20,000 total for any one accident. Maine and New York have the highest plan limits with coverages of $20/40/10 in Maine and $25/50/10 in the latter. The majority of state plans do not offer collision, comprehensive, or medical coverages.

The assigned-risk plans are noted for their high loss

ratios. This, of course, is to be expected. The insurers cannot place many of their bad risks in one classification and expect this group to have the same number of accidents as other groups. There are drivers who do drink, who are repeated violators of the law, and who consistently drive with no regard for the rights of others. However, these driver categories make up 50 percent of those in the assigned-risk plans. There should be no stigma attached to an insured being placed in an assigned-risk plan. The fact is that the other 50 percent of those in the plans are clean risks.

The assigned-risk market is an expensive insurance facility. The following premiums and surcharges are based upon state-wide average premiums for bodily injury and property damage coverage under the assigned-risk and voluntary markets:

ASSIGNED RISKS PAY MORE

State	Assigned Risk Premium	Surcharge	Voluntary Market Premium
California	$186.20	$36.41	$95.45
New York	185.44	70.97	126.72
Ohio	131.35	45.92	96.66
Pennsylvania	145.27	84.83	72.21
South Carolina	142.81	74.90	68.21
Texas	82.07	46.21	69.29
Wisconsin	134.80	67.11	91.12

These are only average premiums and average surcharges. The actual rate of surcharges is from 10 percent of premium to 500 percent. A youthful driver in West Virginia could pay a premium of $1,077 versus a base rate of $234. The insurers, however, despite higher rates, are losing money on their assigned-risk plans.

69

MINORITY GROUPS IN ASSIGNED-RISK PLANS

The practice of discrimination because of race and environment is so subtle that it is difficult to uncover. In 1968, Jerome Kay, member of the Commission on Human Rights in New York, conducted an investigation of the assigned-risk plan in that state. His findings proved conclusively that ghetto residents are being treated as second-class citizens by the insurers. This treatment has persisted, despite the fact that the nonwhite drivers, on the average, have fewer accidents than their white counterparts in the assigned-risk plan.

The commission found that applications for ghetto residents were coded, or that merely the possession of a Spanish-sounding name was reason for denying coverage. The few agents and brokers who submitted numerous nonwhite applications found that the insurers dropped their accounts. The companies claimed that these agents and brokers were submitting business that was no longer profitable and therefore had to be dismissed from the companies' accounts. An insurance executive said that because ghetto residents have limited intelligence and a limited command of the English language, they are unable to protect themselves or negotiate when they are involved in an accident. Further, he said that insurance companies hesitated to take cases to court involving minority-group insurance pitted against the white plaintiff or defendant, because juries tend to be sympathetic to white persons.

The extent of this discrimination is evident from a review of the assigned-risk population. In 1968, New York had a population that was 90.9 percent white and 9.5 percent nonwhite. The assigned-risk plan was comprised of 70.2 percent nonwhite and 29.8 percent white.

It is incredible that such practices as these are allowed to exist, and there is reason enough to believe that the same discrimination goes on in every other state. There is some evidence that Chicago and Detroit are particularly bad in this respect. New York has recently passed a law requiring insurers to insure anyone who has a valid driver's license and who can pay his premium.

THE HIGH RISK MARKET

The high-risk market is the burial ground for the castoffs of the insurance companies. Here the young, the old, the poor, and the sick vie for insurability with the best and the worst of the insurers.

There are two types of insurers in this market: the affiliates of the standard insurers and the independent specialists. State Farm, through its affiliate, State Farm General Casualty Insurance Company, offers auto insurance in this market. If the high-risk market was confined to this company, high-risk policyholders would have little to complain about. But there are other companies, 117 of them, that are something else again. Allstate's affiliate, National Emblem, Travelers', Charter Oak, and the independents—Reserve, Mission, and Yosemite Insurance companies—among the top ten in this market, offer less than they should or could. The real villains, however, are the smaller, independent companies that produce more than half of the premium volume. These companies offer insurance at high prices with limited coverage. Unfortunately, most drivers never realize just how limited their coverage is until they are forced into using it.

In 1968, the top ten companies wrote over $251 million in high-risk premiums. State Farm, the largest, wrote $68 million in premiums and sustained losses of over $10 million. In comparison, State Farm insured over 10.7 million motorists in their standard group with a premium volume

71

of over $1 billion. The underwriting loss here was only $13.5 million. To illustrate this even more dramatically: 10.7 million motorists cost State Farm $13.5 million while 458,000 high-risk motorists cost them $10.7 million. Many independents actually showed a profit. Reserve, Progressive Casualty, and Yosemite Insurance companies showed loss ratios of 55.1, 61.8, and 57.8 respectively.

The point here is that, if the insurers in the normal market say that high-risk motorists are uninsurable at any price, how can the high-risk independents make money? Is it because these companies are offering extremely poor service? If so, why do the state insurance departments allow these companies to operate? The facts seem to validate the contention that the independents are offering poor service. State Farm, for example, is offering high-risk insurance at substantially the same prices as these companies, and it is losing money. The independents must be denying the public proper claims settlement.

The loss ratios of the smaller high-risk specialists, in some cases, seem very low. Many of these companies are outperforming the standard insurers by considerable margins. In view of the disastrous insolvency record of these companies, it would appear that the reported figures are not always truthful figures. One of the most common tricks these specialists employ is either to understate claims loss reserves, or simply to ignore the claims. This enables the company to show a low loss ratio, which, in turn, creates an inflated surplus. The day of reckoning for these companies occurs when state investigations reveal true loss situations, and because principals of the company have been robbing it blind, there is no surplus. The company is then forced into insolvency, and the policyholders and claimants suffer. Most of these companies are relative newcomers to the insurance business, with more than half of them being formed in the last 15 years.

If these companies, the independent specialists, can be called successful in view of the services they do not provide, then a summarization of these factors might be interesting. Even the standard insurers might take heed.

1. The specialists expend large amounts of money in promoting their services to the public. Newspaper ads in the motor-vehicle section of newspapers seem to be their favorite location. The ads these companies use might be called vigorous, to say the least. The favorite headlines are "NO MONEY DOWN" or "WE INSURE ANYONE."

2. The specialists offer much broader coverage than most assigned-risk plans. This coverage might, in fact, prove to be a myth, as the fine print usually contains convenient restrictions that the policyholder never bothers to read. It is possible, for instance, that if a policy read "All accidents must be reported to the XYZ Insurance Company within 24 hours. Failure to comply with this provision is ground for denial of insurance coverage," this provision would be administered without qualifcation. Pity the motorist who calls his company one minute late.

3. The specialists offer immediate binding of insurance coverage. The applicant is told what his premiums will be immediately. Assigned-risk plans can take two or more days.

4. The applicant knows the name of the company he is doing business with at once. The assigned-risk plans do not allow for this as any licensed company may assume the risk. The stigma of being in an assigned-risk plan is also eliminated. Though why there should be any stigma at all is a mystery.

5. Agents are active supporters of the high-risk specialist. The commissions paid on this type of business are much higher than standard policy commissions

and almost twice those of the assigned-risk plans. Too, the premium is so much higher that a 25 percent commission on a $600 policy amounts to $150. The commission on a standard policy of 12 percent and an average policy of $200 only amounts to $24. This is incentive enough for any agent to push the unwary insurance applicant into a high-risk company without any cause.

6. The specialists have developed a premium-financing scheme which allows them to be more competitive with their rates while making up the difference through interest charges of 30 percent or more. The majority of assigned-risk plans require payment in full within 30 days.

7. The specialists offer various good-driver discounts, which the assigned-risk plans do not. The discounts may turn out to be illusory, if the premium is financed.

Some of the specialists, of course, are not guilty of any flagrant practices, and some of them accept clean risks at rates only slightly above those of IRB rates. But the applicant forced into the high-risk market must be very wary of every company. Before purchasing a policy, the applicant should read over very carefully what the policy contains. If the wording is confusing, take it to an attorney and have him read it over and explain all of the provisions in the policy. Most attorneys will do this for a nominal fee, and it could save the applicant grief if he were to have an accident and find he was not covered. The most important factor in purchasing insurance from a high-risk specialist is to shop around. The wary shopper might find himself with a saving of from 10 to 50 percent for just obtaining prices from three or four specialists. A youthful driver with three motor-vehicle violations and one accident will find coverage available at prices ranging from $392 to $807. All that is required is a little patience.

AGENTS

Just what services did agents perform in 1970 that justified motorists paying them $1.6 billion for their auto insurance? An insurance agent is supposedly the liaison between the insurance company and the policyholder. For many years there existed a certain rapport between the agent and his client. He was the friendly man who took care of all those impossible forms; he told the motorist what he should have in the form of coverage, made out the bill, and that was all there was to it. If one of his clients had an accident, he was sympathetic and again helped to fill out those impossible forms, even telling his client what not to say. In those days, auto insurance cost appreciably less than it does now, and the client was not aware, nor did he care, that his agent *was not* the insurance company. In the early fifties things began to change. The direct writers began to make inroads into the insurance business.

The direct writers are those companies that do not rely upon the independent agency system or brokers to market their insurance. These companies have their own sales forces, and because of the volume of business written through these salaried representatives, they are able to offer discounts of 10 to 30 percent under standard rates. Companies like State Farm Mutual, Nationwide, and Allstate are the principal direct writers. There are other companies that offer auto insurance through the mails and advertisements, and do not have any sales personnel at all. These companies are United Services Automobile Association, Government Employees Insurance Company, and numerous other smaller companies. All of these direct-writing companies have experienced tremendous growth in the last 20 years. Just these five companies represent 25 percent of the total auto insurance written.

Twenty years ago, State Farm and Allstate together wrote under 6 percent of the total auto-insurance market. Once more, all of these direct writers are making handsome profits while their brothers, writing through agents, are complaining that they are not making as much profit as they used to make.

Companies like Aetna, Travelers, and Continental fall back slightly each year, and it will not be too long before their positions of prominence in the automobile insurance world will be usurped by the younger, more daring companies. These companies must place a good deal of the blame on agents for their fall from glory. The truth that all of these companies must face sooner or later is that the insurance agent is a luxury the automobile insurer and the policyholder can no longer afford. Automobile insurance has become a very expensive necessity, if one is to drive. It is not difficult to believe that the insurance applicant would take the trouble to understand a little more about the auto insurance and fill out his own forms if it would save him $50 or more.

In this era of mass communication, it is not unreasonable to expect that an insurer use a little imagination and market auto insurance over the television networks. The potential of 20 or 30 million viewers during one sponsored program would seem to have far more appeal than being locked into a few thousand agents, and far less expensive, too. There is no reason why the mails could not be utilized. United Services Automobile Association is one of the finest companies in the country, and it uses the mails exclusively. The insurers must realize that the motorists want to save money and that new and innovative marketing systems must be used. The majority of motorists today are enlightened enough to be able to think and choose for themselves; they simply do not need an expensive, friendly man to fill out forms for them.

Even so, the agent's commission would not be as much of a burden as it is if it were only a one-time expense—that is, if the fee were paid to secure insurance with a company for the first time. Once a policyholder is insured with a company, renewals should be automatic with the simple payment of the premium. There is no need, as is done today, for the agent to collect these exorbitant commissions year in and year out.

Another technique that would save the policyholder appreciable sums of money, in most cases, is the mass marketing of auto insurance. The selling of group insurance by the accident and health insurers has certainly benefited policyholders, and the same technique could be applied to the auto-insurance field. Commissioner Karl Herrmann of the State of Washington recently announced his acceptance of mass marketing when he said:

> In announcing this decision, I would not want the citizens of this state to overestimate its effect. It is but a step which should result in lower premiums to a limited number of insureds. However, I consider it to be an important step, if for no other reason than that it demonstrates that imagination and innovation have a place in the insurance industry and can bring about savings to the public.

As might be expected, the independent agents and brokers in Washington quickly requested and received a stay of the commissioner's subsequent order. This type of action by agents is now a forgone conclusion when any legislation concerning mass marketing of auto insurance is introduced. It is not enough that the motoring public could save up to 20 percent or more and that it would help insurers to remain competitive; the agents do not want any laws or regulations that will threaten their incomes. For many years agents have been successful in preventing mass marketing of auto insurance. Further, they have successfully initiated and supported bills through their legislative lackeys that have prevented the vast majority of group auto plans from becoming a reality. A recent confidential letter to independent agents in Connecticut over their defeat of a viable mass marketing bill follows:

VICTORY IS SWEET

You did it again! Following our urgent appeal in the last Bulletin for help in securing passage of the "open competition bill," HB 7101, and the mass merchandising guidelines bill, HB 8616, *you really went to work* and contacted your local Senators and Representatives. Your personal visits, phone calls and other messages did the job. . . .

Then it was well past the proverbial (and also literal) eleventh hour on the last night of the session, when the Senate approved HB 8616 by a one-vote margin, 17-16. Since the House had already approved the bill it is now in the hands of the Governor and should be signed into law. . . . The bill approves mass merchandising only when there are 700 or more members with at least 70 per cent participation in the plan. *Companies have indicated that they won't and can't write mass merchandising on such a basis!* So once again our hats are off to the independent agents of the state who have proved (as you have in the past) that when we work together there is nothing that cannot be accomplished.

Here is a case of agents working together to help pass a bill that is virtually useless, and, of course, they knew it all along. This action by the Connecticut agents once more brings home the power of these men in the halls of the state legislatures. It will probably take federal action to bring about a group-insurance bill for all of the states.

The University of Pennsylvania, however, is currently in its fourth year as a group auto subscriber to the Insurance Company of North America (INA). This year over 5,000 policyholders are expected to participate in the program at an average savings per individual of 15 percent. Too, the premium is deducted throughout the course of the year under the payroll-deduction process. INA offers home-owners, marine, and even credit-card insurance to the university personnel along with the usual auto-insurance coverage. All risks are insured, but some risks are rated differently from others. Prior driving experience is the basis for all rates. INA is very happy with the plan, but the savings of 15 percent and the plan's availability under the payroll deduction process makes the insurance buyers even more pleased.

Pennsylvania is one of the few states that allows for mass merchandising of insurance. The agents in that state did provide considerable opposition to the plan several years ago, but now they have become resigned to the fact that this is the way insurance will have to be sold in that state in the future. What some agents are beginning to understand is that, if they are to survive, they will have to offer a complete line of financial services to their communities. Such features as mutual-fund investment, complete estate planning, and other financial services will have to be part of the agent's competitive arsenal if he is to survive in the future. The one-man shop is quickly being replaced in some areas with large agencies capable of offering these services.

It is extremely difficult to justify such a large portion of the premium dollar to the agents. A figure of just 7 percent in commissions for the first year of an auto policy with a reduction to 1 percent for each year following would seem far more reasonable. Allowing for mass merchandising, to be marketed by the super agency and the high sales volume possible through such organization, the agents would not lose, and the policyholders would gain. Extensive training programs and strict licensing would also curb other abuses, such as lack of knowledge and counseling ability, and dishonesty.

Dishonesty has become a large problem among insurance agents throughout the country. Each month heavy fines and license revocations are imposed upon these wayward agents. The principal offense committed by these men appears to be the failure to remit premiums to the insurers. A practice that affects the policyholder is that of counseling a policyholder to make a claim against the insurer under the policyholder's collision coverage (with the $100 deductible) instead of a comprehensive claim. The policyholder is usually ignorant of his coverage and follows the advice of his agent. The insurance company saves the deductible, and the agent's balance sheet with the insurer reflects a lower loss. This last type of problem should not be construed as a major practice; the vast majority of agents would never be guilty of such conduct. Nevertheless, these things do occur, and it is up to the agents themselves to police their own fraternity.

PART

THE POLICYHOLDER AND
THE PRESENT SYSTEM

THE CLAIM AND THE CLAIMANT

Accidents must have a cause, and the cause is human, goes a popular notion, especially when an auto is involved. Long before automobiles there were horses and wagons, and they used the streets, in many instances the same streets, that autos use today. A runaway team of horses pulling a large wagon could cause considerable damage before being brought under control, and accidents of this kind occurred regularly. Cases were brought before the civil courts, much as they are today, in order to decide questions of fault. The system worked well enough then, and a whole body of laws concerning negligence developed.

In the early days of the automobile, when an accident occurred, the same negligence laws governing the wagons were used to determine fault. The wagons are gone now, and the country is paved from one end to the other with highways for the benefit of the motoring public. An elaborate system of repair shops, dealers, parts-supply houses, and service stations have evolved to serve the automobile and driver. The cars of today are the science-fiction vehicles of 60 years ago, but today's negligence laws are still keeping pace with the horse and wagon of yesterday.

It is absolutely essential that every motorist understand this fact: the negligence laws governing the liability of drivers are old, outmoded, inhumane, and unjust. When a motorist is involved in an accident, he can be judged contributorily negligent if his windshield is cracked, if his windshield wipers do not work properly, if he does not use his seat belts, if he has a broken head or tail light, if he is not wearing glasses, and a hundred more situations. Contributory negligence has been the bane of the motoring public for years. Insurance companies will go to any lengths to prove contributory negligence, because if it is proved, the insurer is not liable for any damages.

In a minor accident, the claimant is not overly concerned with his liability, because usually the accident results only in property damage. The insurer of the driver who is at fault will pay, and the claim is usually settled quickly. But it is the serious accident that causes real concern. It is after the horror of the crash that the doubts and worries begin. The victim asks himself if he will be able to work again, how his wife and children are going to manage, will they have to become welfare cases? He worries about his bills and whether he will lose his house. Questions, doubts, and a thousand fears besiege the accident victim in his moment of truth and at a time when he is least able to cope with them.

Then there is another set of fears having to do with the crash itself. The victim finds it almost impossible to remember what happened. His first thought is that the other driver was at fault—he had to have been. Then he will doubt, and the thought begins to plague him that perhaps he was guilty of negligence himself. What if he cannot prove that the other driver was at fault? Suppose *he* is found to be at fault? What then? A lifetime of poverty and sickness, with social workers running his life? What kind of life would that be?

There is no feeling quite like waking in a hospital bed in the middle of the night, hurting all over, still groggy from the effects of sedation, and reliving that last moment before the crash. The feeling of being alone in the world slowly creeps over you, and you want to cry. Then you get hold of yourself and try to be practical, only to drift off into a sleep filled with screeching brakes, torn metal, and pain. The nightmare never seems to end, and you feel destined to relive that moment for the rest of your life, over and over again.

This is what happens in a serious accident. What does the insurance industry do for these victims? Fortunately, there is a recent study available that will tell us. The Department of Transportation commissioned Westat Research, Inc., with the help of the Bureau of the Census to make the most comprehensive study ever undertaken of the seriously injured auto-accident victim. The DOT said in its foreword to the publication of this study:

> Although the report of Westat Research, Inc., set out in its entirety in these two volumes must be properly credited to its authors, it would be inappropriate for the Department of Transportation to reserve its judgment about this report. It is without question the most comprehensive and carefully conducted study of the plight of people injured by motor vehicles ever produced and no solution to the myriad problems of the compensation system is possible without a thorough understanding of its implications.

The principal focus of the study centered on the economic losses per individual or family due to serious injury or death from an auto accident. A serious injury was defined as one where medical cost, excluding hospital, was $500 or more, or two weeks or more of hospitalization; or, if working, three weeks or more of missed work, or, if not working, six weeks or more of missed normal activity.

The accident data was collected from police departments, motor-vehicle departments, and sheriff's offices throughout the country. From this data, 1,435 accident victims were interviewed in person. In addition, releases were obtained from the victims to authorize doctors, lawyers, and hospitals to provide verification information. Only those victims who were not involved in any pending litigation concerning their accidents were interviewed.

The concept of economic loss included hospital, doctors, nurses, therapists, medicines, ambulance service, prosthesis, and property damage to the individual's or family car. Wage loss was computed using actual loss up to the time of the interview, and a future projection was estimated for lost wages of the victims. No adjustment was made for future wage increases over the time period of the wage loss. Economic loss also included other actual expenses, such as transportation costs, funeral expenses, household help, and other miscellaneous expenses. Future losses included medical expenses in addition to wage losses. In short, the study attempted to project those losses that a family or an individual would sustain in addition to those actual losses already incurred.

The seriously injured, according to the report, suffered an average loss of about $4,200 up to the date of the interview (18 to 30 months after the accident), and an estimated average future loss of $4,100. These losses were primarily wage losses.

Economic losses sustained by fatality cases were estimated at $2,300, mostly in the form of funeral costs. Their average discounted future earnings, however, were $87,000, which does not include personal and family losses.

About 47 percent of seriously injured accident victims received reparations through a tort action. This means that presumably 47 percent of these victims were adjudged to be faultless in their accidents. Those at fault could only collect for their medical expenses under their auto-insurance medical policies or some collateral source of insurance such as Blue Cross. The auto insurer does not pay claims for liability when the insured is found to be at fault in an auto accident. If both parties are found at fault in a collision, neither can recover from his auto insurer for liability. We can estimate, then, that 53 percent of seriously injured traffic victims are at fault, guilty of contributory negligence, or cannot find a negligent defendant.

For those victims whose losses exceed $5,000, the amount of reparations compared to losses begins to widen. Thus an average loss of $6,632 receives on the average only $5,521 from all sources of recovery. For those victims with losses averaging $16,482, reparations amounted to $9,681, and for the extreme case, an average loss of $71,000 only brought the victim $12,718 in reparations from all sources.

For those victims who received reparations under tort recovery about 60 percent of their actual losses were reimbursed by the auto insurers.

For those victims who sustain losses under $5,000, their recovery was substantially better: 69.6 percent of victims suffering losses averaging $332 received more than twice their loss from all sources. For those whose average loss ranged between $762 and $3,486 the reparations averaged from 150 percent of the loss to an amount approximately equal to the loss.

This report clearly tells us that we do not receive the benefits we pay for in premiums. Most of us can recover from the less severe types of accidents in a relatively short time, and our losses will not be so great that we cannot make them up in a year or two. But it is the serious accident that leaves us disabled or even hospitalized for a prolonged period of time which we cannot afford. This sort of loss is the reason we purchase auto insurance.

We have far more accidents of a less severe nature that involve bodily injury, and of these only 47 percent actually recover their losses through initiating a tort action. The importance of establishing a clear case of negligence on the part of the other driver, a manufacturer, a government agency, or a property owner in an automobile accident is necessary if the claimant is to collect anything at all from his adversary's insurer or the guilty party himself. This is the system, and we are forced to prove our own innocence without the slightest possibility of there being any guilt on our part. The system promotes dishonesty, fraud, and perjury, but it is the system, and we must live with it, at least for the present.

The claimant in an auto accident must be prepared to play a game that has become almost a science. He must deal with hospitals, doctors, insurance adjusters, and investigators, lawyers, and his own greed. Eventually he may have to go to court and present his case to a bored judge and an emotional jury. Most importantly, the claimant must be aware of every pitfall that awaits him if he is to be successful in winning his case.

The events leading up to an accident are of primary importance because it is here that the basis for liability will be determined. First, did you, the operator of the vehicle, act in a prudent manner? Did you do anything unreasonable? Did you observe all traffic laws? Was there anything unusual happening at the time of the accident, such as a construction project? Were all lane markings evident? Were all traffic signs clearly visible? Had you noticed anything different in how your car operated? Did the brakes function properly? The steering? When was the last time you had a mechanic work on your car? Were there any witnesses? And finally, what did the driver of the other vehicle do? All of these questions are of paramount importance and should be noted down as soon as possible.

88

Regardless of how much in the right you may think you are, always proceed on the premise that you may not be. Every factor is important.

Two drivers collided at the intersection, and each claimed the light was green. After considerable delay and testimony from witnesses, it was established that the traffic light was not functioning properly and that it had been green for both parties. Unfortunately, the statute of limitations in many states is only 60 days for actions against any branch of government. Some states allow even less time. Because the malfunctioning of the traffic light was the cause of the accident, neither driver could collect from the other for their liability claims. A suit could only have been brought against the municipal government for their negligence.

A store located on the corner of a busy intersection installed a large new awning. A car driven by a man who had never been in the area before entered the intersection without stopping and collided with another vehicle. The man was cited for failure to observe a stop sign. Later the man protested that he had not seen the stop sign, and because he had been taken to the hospital in an unconscious state, he had not been able to determine if there had been a sign. It seemed to be a clear case of negligence on the part of the driver who had failed to observe the stop sign. The man, however, was adamant in his denial that there had been a stop sign.

One rainy afternoon, he returned to the scene of the accident and found the stop sign. The man's insurer paid the claim of the other driver and paid for the medical expenses under the guilty driver's auto medical coverage. Several weeks later the man happened to be driving through the same area again, and this time he noticed that the awning was down and that the stop sign was not visible. He immediately started suit against the owner of the store for his negligence in obstructing the stop sign. Another case involving an apparently guilty driver recently occurred. The driver in this incident was in heavy traffic approaching a red light. He applied his brakes, and the car would not stop. The driver smashed into the rear end of a car stopped for the light. The driver tried to explain that his brakes had failed, but no one would listen. The police officer on the scene issued him a citation alleging reckless driving. Three weeks before the man had his garage replace the master cylinder in the braking system. Upon investigation, the man found that the new cylinder was defective. He sued the garage and won a settlement for the garage's negligence. All of these cases point out the many factors that can be involved in an accident.

Over half of the states have guest laws which provide that under most conditions a guest passenger may not bring suit against the owner or operator of a motor vehicle. The law is inhumane and unjust, and there is no reason why the states should not move to abolish it immediately. The guest law of the State of Iowa is similar to the guest laws in most states and reads as follows:

> State of Iowa—Liability to guest in motor vehicle.
>
> Owner or operator shall not be liable for any damages to any passenger or person riding in said vehicle as a guest or by invitation and not for hire unless damage "caused as a result of influence of intoxicating liquors or the reckless driving by him of such vehicle."

Even for the guest of the drunken or reckless driver there are conditions that have to be met in the courts. Did the victim, in any way, show his concern for the reckless manner in which the vehicle was being operated? In other words, if you, the guest, did not warn the driver that he was behaving in a reckless manner and ask him to stop the car and let you out, you would be guilty of contributory negligence. Silence, in this case, would indicate your approval of the driver's actions.

On the night of April 11, 1964, in Iowa City, Iowa, a Volkswagen traveling at an excessive rate of speed went off the road, rolling over twice and throwing its occupants clear. Both passengers were killed. This is the way this accident might appear in the morning paper, but an investigation of such a story might reveal a situation similar to what follows:

Steve Brown was 23 years old and mentally retarded. He had suffered oxygen starvation at birth which had caused permanent brain damage. Steve could carry on a conversation and do most things for himself. The lad was well liked, and one of his greatest pleasures was to be allowed to go bowling. On the night of April 11, Fred Grant, a roomer in the Brown household, asked permission to borrow the Browns' Volkswagen so that he could take Steve bowling. This had been a practice of the pair for some time. Mr. Brown handed over the keys, and the two were off.

They arrived at the bowling alley and found that they would have to wait some time before they could get a lane. The two left the bowling alley, presumably to go for a ride and to come back later when the bowling alley was less crowded. Fred Grant drove onto the main highway and proceeded to accelerate. The speed limit was 40 miles per hour. Fred pushed the car to its limit, attaining a speed in excess of 80 miles per hour, the police later estimated. As he approached a long curve, the car hit the shoulder, and Fred fought to control the car, only to have it turn over and slide across the road where it turned over again. Fred was thrown clear for a distance of 60 feet and was killed instantly. Steve was thrown 125 feet and died 30 minutes later at the Iowa University Hospital.

In any accident where someone is hurt badly or is killed,

91

the family and friends can only feel shock and grief. After the initial grief is passed, questions arise. Why was Fred driving at such a high rate of speed, knowing that Steve would be frightened? Why did they not stay in the bowling alley? All of this conjecture, of course, does not answer the questions. But in this case, everything pointed to the reckless operation of the motor vehicle by Fred Grant with no apparent reason unless he had wanted to commit suicide. The man had just lost his job, and he had been divorced a short time previously. Could he have wanted to end his own life and, perhaps feeling sorry for Steve whom he loved as a young brother, to take them both out of the misery of the world?

Two years later the case went to trial. The defense attorney for the insurance company argued that the guest law applied and that the insurer was not liable for any damages. The plaintiff attorney argued that the guest law could not apply as the car had obviously been driven at an excessive rate of speed, which could only be construed as reckless driving. The defense attorney, using every wile he possessed, told the jury, "Now ladies and gentlemen of the jury, you and I both know that we all drive a little over the speed limit at times, don't we?" The implication here is clear. The attorney was trying to set the idea in the jurors' minds that the car might have been traveling at a speed in excess of the speed limit, but that it was a common occurrence, and certainly no accident could occur as a result of it. The jury, of course, would have to agree, because everyone does exceed the speed limit at one time or another. There had to be another cause for the accident, and the attorney was ready. He suggested that the only way the accident could have happened was if the passenger, Steve, had tried to wrench the wheel away from the driver. The jury bought the argument, and the defense won. The insurer was not liable for damages.

The Browns were shocked at the outcome of the trial. Many others were as well. The staff psychologist at the state university, who had been counseling Steve, was shocked. He stated that in his opinion Steve was incapable of making a move such as the defense attorney had suggested. A violent action of any kind was simply not in his nature.

The injustice and inhumanity of the guest law is practiced at will in over half of the states. Can we allow such inhumanity to continue?

Another aspect of the negligence law defies reason: in the case of the accident where the driver of one of the vehicles is drunk, the driver of the other vehicle, if he was only slightly negligent, cannot collect any damages unless he can prove that the drunken driver was grossly negligent.

Highway 17 stretches down through southern Virginia into North Carolina. It is a two-lane road with drainage ditches on either side of the road. The road is dark at night with no lights visible for miles. Two young sailors had picked up two girls in Portsmouth, Virginia, and were off for a ride. None of the occupants was drinking, and they were traveling along at a fair rate of speed. The driver of the car, Larry Bentz, noticed a pair of headlights off in the distance which seemed to be weaving across the road. He slowed down to about 40 miles per hour and pulled his car to the right of the road as far as he could until the tires were riding on the shoulder. Larry was afraid that the driver of the other car might not see him properly because his left front headlight was not working. The cars came closer, and now Larry was sure the driver of the other car was drunk. He slowed down to 30 miles per hour and kept as far to the right as possible. The cars met in a head-on collision. Larry's front left wheel was torn off as the car turned over and slid into the drainage ditch.

Larry was unhurt and managed to drag himself out of

93

the car. His three passengers were moaning and crying behind him as he climbed the embankment. The other car was stopped in the middle of the road, and Larry ran up to the window on the driver's side to ask for help. There were five other people in the car, and Larry could smell the unmistakable odor of liquor. The driver asked Larry if there was anyone hurt, and Larry replied that it appeared everyone in the car was hurt, and he needed help to drag them out. Larry turned and ran back to his car and started to pull the girl in the front seat out of the car. She was unconscious. He heard the sound of a car starting and saw that the other car was driving off, with a sound of dragging metal and a tire rubbing against a fender. Larry glanced at the license number of the car and went back to work.

The police came on the scene shortly thereafter and managed to pull all of the occupants out of the car. Ambulances were summoned, and all three passengers were taken to the hospital in serious condition. The police noted in their accident report that the point of impact of the two cars was three feet from the center line of the road. The driver of the other car had come three feet into Larry's lane and hit him.

The victims all sustained serious injuries. One of the girls had a fractured arm and a concussion; the other sailor had fractured ribs and a fractured collarbone; the second girl suffered serious internal injuries, and it was learned that she had been pregnant and had aborted. The driver of the other car was apprehended 35 minutes after the accident occurred and was charged with drunken driving, driving to endanger, leaving the scene of an accident, and a few more charges thrown in for good measure. The man was also a sailor and had been at a party.

The case came to trial a year later, and the defense attorney contended that Larry was guilty of contributory negligence because his left front headlight was broken. The

94

plaintiff's attorney showed that the driver of the other car had, in fact, been intoxicated, and that he was barely able to walk when apprehended. The court ruled in favor of contributory negligence, and the case was over.

Larry and the passengers of his car had to pay for their own damage, and Larry was further obliged to pay the medical expenses of the two girls who were penniless. There were no further actions against Larry by the girls.

There is no doubt that Larry was in the wrong in driving his automobile with a broken headlight. In view of the circumstances and his defensive actions, the accident would not have occurred if the driver of the other vehicle had not been intoxicated. But the fact of contributory negligence, no matter how slight, is enough to lose a case.

The insurance adjuster is an important factor in accident settlements. If he makes an appearance, the claimant can be assured that his case is a serious one. Most minor cases are processed through the mail, and the details are handled routinely. In the case of a serious accident, the adjuster is on the scene as quickly as possible to ascertain what actually happened at the scene of the accident. He represents the insurer, and to him the claimant is the enemy. His greatest desire is to settle the case quickly and for a fraction of its worth.

One word of advice here: always tell an adjuster the truth, but do not tell him too much. Statements made by a victim to an adjuster can end up haunting him for the rest of his life.

LAWYERS AND THE CLAIMANT

Lawyers, as guardians of the law, play a vital role in the preservation of society. The fulfillment of this role requires an understanding by lawyers of their relationship with and function in our legal system. A consequent obligation of lawyers is to maintain the highest standards of ethical conduct.

—Legal Ethics Code

Can anyone doubt that the practice of law is an ancient and honorable profession—that its practitioners are an invaluable asset to a civilized society? We, the general public, hold the legal profession in high regard, and our confidence in the law itself is in direct relationship to our confidence in the bar. There are corporate attorneys, patent attorneys, tax, maritime, and trademark attorneys. There are criminal lawyers, probate and liability lawyers, and there are ambulance chasers.

The ambulance chaser is our concern here, for he is the mocker of judicial ethics and a cancer eating away at the respectability of our courts. He is the shame of his profession, and the curse of the auto-accident claimant.

The *New York Law Journal* publishes disciplinary proceedings against recalcitrant lawyers. The journal of December 8, 1969, carried the following proceeding.

The respondent in this case was a lawyer who had been admitted to the New York Bar in June of 1956. The charges against the lawyer were:

(1) that he had attempted unlawfully to influence a police officer in connection with the performance of his duties;

(2) that he had willfully deceived a justice of the Supreme Court in order to induce approval of a proposed compromise of infant's personal injury claims and, in connection therewith, altered affidavits;

(3) that he had solicited negligence cases;

(4) that he had maliciously instituted malpractice actions against two separate physicians;

96

(5) that he had wrongfully attempted to obtain legal fees in excess of that awarded him by the Workmen's Compensation Board.

The journal lists 13 separate specifications to these charges. Some of the more flagrant were that the respondent had "counseled, advised and urged" the police officer to destroy and alter an official police accident report, and to fabricate a false report. He was also found guilty of "advising and urging" the police officer to participate in an unlawful scheme to defraud an insurance company. The officer was to claim falsely that he had been inside the unoccupied police car which had been struck by the respondent's client and to claim falsely that as a result thereof he had sustained a serious personal injury, and that in connection with said scheme the respondent offered to represent the police officer as his attorney to prosecute the claim for personal injuries and advised that, if the criminal charge lodged against his client were withdrawn or dismissed, the respondent would obtain his client's cooperation in defrauding the insurance company.

The respondent urged the police officer to go immediately to a local hospital. When the officer stated that there was nothing wrong with him and indicated that this would pose some difficulty in an examination, the respondent stated: "I'll tell you what is wrong with you. . . . I would complain as follows: ringing sounds in your ears, spots in front of your eyes, dizzy headaches—you banged your head on the wheel or the window—you don't remember, you're nauseous, you've got pains in your back, pains in your left elbow and your left knee. That's enough." The respondent then gave the officer the name of a local doctor whom he was to see the morning following his appearance at the hospital, stating, "Just tell him that I told you to see him. And if you feel like

97

spending some time in the hospital, he'll put you in." The respondent added: "I'd go sick right now and shoot up to the hospital emergency room. Give him all your symptoms; even though they don't buy that, as long as they make a record of all your symptoms."

When the respondent ascertained that the officer had struck his finger with a hammer three weeks prior to the conversation, the respondent stated: "You show him that, and you tell him that it's from the accident. You banged your finger on you don't know what—on the wheel." When the respondent informed the officer as to the possible recovery from the insurance company, the respondent stated: "The maximum you can get here is ten grand," and that it "depends on how long you want to stay in the hospital." The respondent was confronted with a tape recording of the statements above, and he conceded the accuracy of the tape recording and the transcript. Some of the other specifications were not proved, but the majority of them were. The respondent was disbarred from the practice of law for his actions.

In another case in the summer of 1970, the respondent was found guilty of setting up a referral system from tow-car operators, automobile repairmen, and others for auto-accident cases. The respondent was also found to have arrived at the home of an accident victim the day after an accident uninvited, to solicit him as a client. This attorney was suspended from the practice of law for five years.

This writer knows personally a young lady who was involved in an accident over two years ago, in which she and her child suffered minor injuries and damages to her car of $400 to $500. Sharon contacted a lawyer who agreed to take the case. Liability in this case was unquestionable, and a statement to that effect had been taken by Sharon at the scene of the accident from the other driver. Sharon was told to go and see a certain doctor. She replied that she had her own physician and that her union would pick up the bill. The lawyer insisted that she see his doctor. Sharon was given a brief examination and was given an elastic bandage to wrap around her lower back (which she had fractured a few years earlier). She was advised to stay at home for at least a week and not to go to work. At the time, Sharon's earnings were about $250 per week.

One year later the lawyer called her in to his office and asked that she pay him $200 toward his expenses in the case. She refused, stating that the case was being paid under a contingency arrangement that he had agreed to previously. The lawyer then said that he would not handle the case. Sharon stood fast in her refusal and left his office.

Another year went by, and she received a release and a check for $190. In a separate bill the lawyer listed his expenses: $100 to doctor, $210 for the lawyer's fee, and the balance of the out-of-court settlement of $500, or $190, to Sharon. This would appear to be a case of outright thievery. Not only had the lawyer tried to intimidate Sharon, but he had gone on to make a settlement without her knowledge, and for an amount that was less than her loss.

According to Jerome E. Carlin,* between the years 1951 and 1962 there have been an average of 1,500 complaints a year filed against lawyers with the Grievance Committee of the Association of the Bar of the City of New York. Over 60 percent of these charges involve client neglect or disputes over fees. All but 5 percent of these are disposed of informally by the staff of the committee.

Each year, on the average, about 60 cases are brought to a formal hearing before a panel of the Grievance Com-

*Ethics and Legal Profession: A study of Social Control in the New York City Bar, Jerome E. Carlin (unpublished).

mittee. In the 11-year period a little over one fifth of these cases have been dismissed; in 37 percent of the cases the lawyer in question was admonished, and in 40 percent of these cases recommendations for prosecution were made. Prosecution is a restricted affair in which a hearing before a court-appointed referee is conducted, and final adjudication is made by the Appellate Division of the Supreme Court. An average of about 19 percent of these cases have reached final adjudication.

New York has more lawyers than any other city in the country, and the variety and complexity of the cases tried there would certainly allow for the number of complaints received. Further, it is understandable that most of these complaints are unfounded, due to the ignorance of the complainant regarding legal procedure. Each state bar association is responsible for the degree of severity with which lawyers are investigated and prosecuted. There is nothing more humiliating for the bar and its membership than to see headlines exclaiming over the wrongdoing of some ambulance chaser.

The role of a lawyer in an auto negligence case can be an important one, and in a great many cases, it can be an unnecessary one. Generally, if a question of negligence is raised by the insurer, or the plaintiff feels that the issue is not clear, a lawyer is unquestionably necessary. In the unusual case, where the issues might be of a precedent-setting nature, a lawyer is necessary. But in the average case a lawyer is not only unnecessay, but the claimant receives less money after all expenses are deducted and fees are paid than if he had settled with an insurer privately. The following table will illustrate this amply:

DOES IT PAY TO HAVE A LAWYER?*

Ratio of Recovery to Economic Loss

Total Economic Loss	For those retaining counsel	For those without counsel
$1- 499	3.05	2.79
500- 999	1.77	1.65
1,000- 1,499	1.48	2.27
1,500- 2,499	1.18	1.26
2,500- 4,999	1.06	.68
5,000- 9,999	.73	.43
10,000-24,999	.45	.37
25,000 and over	.11	.01

The above figures indicate the ratio of payments for economic loss to amounts actually lost. Simply stated, the figure 3.05 in column headed "for those retaining counsel" means that victims with losses in the range of $1 to $499 recovered 3.05 times their actual economic loss. The column headed "for those without counsel" corresponds to the previous column and indicates that the victims without counsel recovered .26 less.

The differences are far more apparent in the $1,000 to $1,499 loss bracket where the claimant without counsel received .79 more than his counterpart who retained counsel. In no way must this table be construed to mean that accident victims should never retain an attorney. It could well be that many of the claimants with counsel who received settlements, may never have received anything at all, particularly if the question of liability was hotly contested. It is also obvious that many cases of liability are not contested, making a lawyer's services superfluous.

---

*Department of Transportation study, Economic Consequences of Automobile Accident Injuries, Vol. 1. Washington, D.C.: U.S. Government Printing Office, April 1970.

The settlement amounts shown in the table would show a far greater difference if lawyers' fees and expenses were deducted from the settlement amounts shown. Most authorities estimate that attorneys' fees average 35.5 percent of gross payments. In addition, the average expense generated in a case amounted to $250 per suit filed. These expenses amount to an additional 3.2 percent of total payments to all claimants. The total cost to bring the average case to a point where suit is filed is 38.7 percent, of the gross settlement. This is obviously a very large amount of money to pay for legal services.

When one compares average settlement amounts with no attorney to settlement amounts with an attorney, the question must arise as to the value of having the present insurance system subsidize the legal profession's liability specialists. The argument raised by the trial lawyers' associations is that, if it were not for the trial lawyers, claims settlements would be much lower than they are today. We might ask, What difference does it make if it is the lawyers who are reaping most of the increases? The public-relations efforts of the trial lawyers are to be commended.

Stephen I. Martin, associate counsel for the National Association of Independent Insurers, writing in *Insurance* magazine, said, "For too many years the operation of the negligence liability system has seemed to be the exclusive preserve of the organized plaintiffs' bar. . . ." Mr. Martin goes on to deplore the tactics of trial lawyers in publicizing the huge jury awards that the press carries so dutifully. These same newspapers seldom mention those cases that are so frequently lost on appeal where the $200,000 award is reduced to $15,000 or even nothing at all. This is understandable due to the lesser sensationalism involved, but it is certainly not to be condoned.

What publicity of this nature does accomplish is to

make the public think that the wealth of insurers is unlimited and that with a "smart lawyer" a claimant can achieve instant wealth. Juries are made out of the public, who have drunk at the fountain of this nonsense and who in turn are influenced to think that there is nothing wrong in a high-award settlement. There are many cases where the high award is not high enough, that is true. But the majority of the cases where the need is greatest go uncompensated or only partially compensated, due to the vagaries of the law and the inability of these same juries to comprehend the issues involved. Too many juries are content to award a man with three children a total settlement of $15,000 for the loss of both his legs, while granting $30,000 to a young lady who sustained a facial scar two inches long.

We never hear about the man who gets nothing in an accident case. Newspapers, looking for the sensational, overlook the everyday tragedy of the uncompensated accident victims.

The high jury awards we hear about are all too often for minor disfigurement. If the trial lawyers could point to major improvements in the compensation of seriously injured accident victims, then we would have cause to laud their efforts. The present insurance and compensation system encourages the bias of witnesses, the theatrics of lawyers, and the emotional decisions of juries. A courtroom is not a place to practice perjury, deceit, falsehoods, intimidation, and theatrics; it is a place for the giving of evidence and objective arguments that can be weighed with a minimum of bias and emotionalism for a just and reasonable verdict.

THE INDEX SYSTEM AND FRAUD

Over 900 property and casualty insurers and self-insurers

are subscribers to the index system. (Self-insurers are companies like Ford Motor Company, General Motors, RCA, the Post Office Department, and certain towns and municipalities.) What the index provides is a storehouse of information concerning 24 million claimants who have been in accidents involving bodily injury and who have sued insurers, towns, auto manufacturers, and the like for damages. Each day, ten regional centers receive and process thousands of claimant cards containing personal and accident information.

The primary purpose of the index is to store and release information to investigators, enabling them to evaluate a claimant's accident history. Frequently, a claimant will forget an accident that happened years before; at least this is the reasoning that is given by the administrators of the index system. What the index actually does is fairly obvious. There are many dishonest claimants, attorneys, and doctors. The index indicates the type of accident, who the attorney or attorneys were, who the doctor was, the course of treatment given by the doctor, and details of the accident.

It is possible for the index to indicate, even if an alias is used, that an accident repeater is being processed. The information is then turned over to the fraud department for investigation. The system is, unfortunately, not automated, and the information-retrieval process is still limited.

Automation would make it possible, for instance, for the index to keep account of every attorney, doctor, and claimant in the country. If a doctor began to show up in the system as being paid inordinately large amounts of money, the system would notify its operators, and the case would then be investigated.

The present system does, however, allow for rather interesting procedures, because each card contains information that classifies a claimant by identifiable characteristics other than his name. Merely a physical description may be enough to associate the claimant doctor or lawyer with another, which in turn would lead to an investigation. The index lists 99 percent of all property and liability insurers as subscribers.

Reliable estimates place a figure of $1.3 billion as the amount insurers paid out in fraudulent claims in 1970. While it is not possible to verify this figure, insurers claim it might be a conservative estimate. The trend, however, indicates that the incidence of fraudulent claims may be decreasing. Improved detection systems and the reluctance of the ordinary motorists to exaggerate or file false claims for fear that their coverage might be canceled, has become a marked factor in this decrease during the latter half of 1970 and the first few months of 1971.

To many, the automobile-insurance industry represents a vast grab bag filled with millions of dollars that are there for the taking. It is not too difficult to rig an accident, and fraud can take as many forms as human ingenuity can invent. In the Bronx, New York, a group of eight were charged with staging accidents with trucks and then collection settlements of between $62.50 and $2,000 from insurers. At least eight insurance companies and 17 out-of-state trucking firms were milked in the scheme.

The group's method of operation was quite simple. Two or more members of the group would drive onto the Cross-Bronx Expressway, a heavily traveled roadway, and wait for an out-of-state truck to appear. They would then maneuver their car in front of the truck and slow down to 15 miles per hour or so. The truck would necessarily have to slow down and would be very close to the car, when the driver of the car would slam on his brakes; the truck driver would not have a chance of avoiding a rear-end collision. The impact would not cause a great deal of vehicle damage, but the occupants would be shaken up considerably. The police would arrive on the scene, make out a report, and the "victims" would seek hospital treatment.

The group would always have a clear-cut case of liability, using the rear-end collision, and by picking on out-of-state trucks they knew that insurers would settle quickly rather than become involved in long and expensive court battles. Several truck drivers lost their jobs because of the accidents, and several more were injured in the collisions. The group collected more than $15,000 in 18 accidents over a 13-month period. One member of the group, carried away with his own cleverness, was alleged to have tried to get a five-year-old boy to go along for a ride with the purpose of getting into an accident. Fortunately, a neighbor overheard the offer and removed the boy to safety.

Police were notified of the increased number of accidents by the insurers along that particular stretch of roadway. Detectives, posing as insurance investigators, finally uncovered the group, and arrests followed.

Doctors and lawyers, it seems, are not immune to the lure of easy money either. In 1969, a ring of seven lawyers, two doctors, one insurance supervisor, and one claims adjuster were all indicted on various charges to defraud the Maryland Casualty Company. To date, two of the lawyers and two doctors have been convicted in fraud conspiracy. The four could face jail terms of up to three years each. Another five of the conspirators pleaded guilty and were fined $1,000 each. In mid-1971, five more persons were tried on similar charges.

A similar scheme in Louisiana with two doctors and five lawyers participating, along with 14 others, came to an end after four years of defrauding 14 insurance companies. This ring faked accidents, but in their exuberance they also used the mails in their scheme. This brought the federal government into the act, and in December of 1970 the case finally came to trial. One defendant, accused of procuring individuals and cars to use in staging fake wrecks, told the court how he cut his arm to make it appear that he had been in a bad wreck. The defendant also stated that, after one staged wreck, he had gone to the doctor's office for heat treatments seven times, the doctor himself being in on this scheme.

Fraud is not confined to professional men like doctors and lawyers; most fraudulent claims are submitted by claimants looking for an extra few dollars and in some instances thousands. An insurer will go to any length to uncover a fraudulent claim. The claimant, for instance, who complains of a severe back injury, no longer able to work because of it, is immediately suspect. Because there are legitimate claims involving back injury, an insurer will look for positive proof to disallow the claim.

The claimant submitting a suspect claim can un-knowingly be the object of some of the most intensive investigative work, and often the results of the investigation reveal fraud. Investigators have a complete bag of tricks to use on the claimant. Cameras concealed in delivery trucks, in rented apartments across the street, or set up for staged incidents are common devices. The claimant, unaware of the hidden surveillance, putters around in his yard, moving trash cans around, or bending down and picking up a coil of garden hose, is caught on film. This film will later be shown at the claimant's trial, and his severe back injury claim proved fraudulent.

The claimant may find himself the object of some female attention. He may go for a walk in the park, and a beautiful blonde will approach him and start a conversation. This leads to a few drinks in a bar and perhaps a hotel room. The camera, of course, is hidden and stays hidden. At the trial, the man is questioned by an attorney as to his activities since his accident. He is asked whether he has been able to work, whether he has been able to carry on a normal sex life, and so forth. The claimant will probably answer that he has been too sick to do anything. Then the film is shown, and the man's true condition is uncovered.

A representative of an insurance-fraud investigating department revealed that the largest administrative loss to the entire insurance industry is the theft of bank drafts. Large insurers have a number of drafts available in strategic locations in each state. These drafts are used to pay claimants, and each draft carries the name of the bank that will honor the drafts.

One San Francisco girl was caught after she had managed to forge and cash some $300,000 worth of drafts. Another San Francisco man set up a dummy savings account using stolen ID and credit cards. The man deposited the drafts in his account; then a short time later he went into the bank and converted the savings account into traveler's checks. Before the man was finally apprehended in Florida, he had succeeded in spending thousands of his stolen dollars.

A ring of brokers selling bank drafts was actually caught in New York several years ago. The ring would steal the drafts and then charge a commission to the people buying the drafts from them. The buyers would then forge the drafts and cash them at will. Banks are liable for forged drafts, but secondary recovery is available to the banks through fidelity bonding companies, who in turn often succeed in recovering from the insurer.

The relationship between attorneys and insurance adjusters is often a financial one. Some attorneys are not averse to paying a kickback to the cooperative adjuster. Often, too, the simple kickback of a few dollars or a new suit for the adjuster grows into an elaborate phony-claims racket involving many thousands of dollars.

A new central investigating unit has been organized by

the insurers for the express purpose of combating fraudulent claims and other fraud in the auto-insurance industry. This organization has its headquarters in Chicago and is being staffed with some of the finest investigators from all parts of the country.

It would seem that a much more efficient information-retrieval system, organized within the index system for the express purpose of uncovering fraud and using automated data processing coupled with a centralized fraud investigative unit, would answer many of the problems. The insurers, too, would like this to happen, but a spokesman for the index explained that computers are simply not sophisticated enough yet to do the job.

In terms of saving the policyholders money, a more efficient index system would allow substantial savings through fraud detection. The system, as it stands today, is possibly the best that can be expected under the circumstances. What we do know is that some 10 percent of claimant dollars paid out are fraudulently acquired. Without the present system, it would be undoubtedly much higher. With a better system, a saving of close to the 10 percent, or some $800 million, could be realized yearly.

THE AUTOMOBILE

You have to care a lot before you deliberately smash a brand-new car into a brick wall to prove a point, and Dr. William Haddon, Jr., has been doing it regularly for the last couple of years. As head of the Insurance Institute for Highway Safety, Dr. Haddon set out to prove that a simple 10-mile-per-hour crash could result in exorbitant repair bills. A filmed report of one crash shows a 1970 Ford Maverick sedan smashing into a barrier at 10 miles per hour. The impact sends a ripple of concussion waves along

109

the front fenders, its bumper caves in, the grille retreats, and the hood crunches up like an accordion. There are other damages inside the hood to the radiator and the fan-blade assembly. The total repair bill came to $427.35. Dr. Haddon filmed other cars with similar results.

The auto insurers have been faced with a problem. Auto-repair costs are skyrocketing, resulting in higher premiums for vehicle-damage coverages. The effort to curb costs at the repair-shop level proved impossible. The only solution was to attack the auto manufacturers. This involved a complete new rate structure and the publication of the names and models of automobiles that were highly damageable.

Some insurers are offering discounts for cars that can withstand a five-mile-per-hour barrier crash with no damage. A discount of 20 percent could mean savings of from $20.80 to $50.21 on vehicle-damage insurance. Allstate says that, if all of its insured cars could meet the crash test, policyholders would save $42.4 million a year.

The principal fault lies in bumper design and quality. Dr. Haddon's group found that the design of bumpers allows scant protection in low-speed crashes. The group tested six 1969 cars by crashing them into a barrier at five miles per hour; the cost of replacing the front bumper and other damages ran as high as $305 and averaged $200.

The insurers claim that a standard bumper height of 20 inches for all cars would further reduce costly damages. Bumpers tend to override in a collision, and today's cars with bumpers of varying heights intensify the problem. At certain speeds a collision between two cars with identical bumper heights would cause little or no damage to the rest of the car, providing, too, that the bumpers were constructed of sturdy material. Some bumpers can be bent with a simple kick or stretched out of shape when the car is jacked up, towed, or hoisted. Ford has promised to

110

introduce all 1972 cars with bumpers of uniform heights. Ford has also acquired an energy-absorbing bumper manufacturer in California, but before these bumpers become standard equipment, Ford says, it is going to try to equip all cars with steel-framed bumpers encased in rubber. The cost and availability of the energy-absorbing bumpers are obviously a major factor in this decision.

Recent styles of automobiles have portions of the car extending over the bumper, further aggravating the minor-collision problems. Spacing in the interior of the car has become extremely tight, to the point that a rear-end collision can cause damage to the radiator. Many $2 parts must be replaced with a $30 or $40 assembly. Head lamps, tail lamps, and interior items are particularly vulnerable in this regard.

High-horsepower cars are another target of the insurers. These cars have a high engine-performance-to-weight ratio and are called "muscle" cars in the industry. The Ford Mustang Boss, Mercury Cougar/Eliminator, Plymouth Sport Fury GT 440, and the Pontiac GTO are muscle cars.

During the past two years, most insurance companies have surcharged the owners of these vehicles some 50 percent. In Cleveland, for instance, liability, collision, and comprehensive insurance on a muscle car was raised from $435 to $650. State Farm has imposed an average 25 percent increase on all insurance coverage for owners of muscle cars. State Farm defines a muscle car as one that will accelerate from 0 to 60 miles per hour in eight seconds.

Many of these cars are being purchased by young, immature drivers with little or no experience in handling cars capable of 120 or more miles per hour. These drivers are not afraid of showing off their cars either; racing stripes, wide-track tires, air scoops, and spoiler to hold down the back end are a common sight.

111

The insurers claim that it takes a certain kind of individual to own a racing machine of the high-performance, muscle type. The driver is usually young and male and has aggressive tendencies. Drivers of this sort, it would appear, try to make up for their lack of maturity with status in the form of a motorized missile.

Not only is accident severity much higher with these cars, but repair costs are appreciably higher too. The average claim cost for adult (immature) drivers in the muscle class is $400, and $436 for male youthful drivers. In contrast, the average repair cost for lesser horsepower cars, according to Senator Hart, is $200.

The following letter from a distraught mother points up some of the difficulties of muscle-car ownership. This letter was reprinted in a transcript of hearings before Senator Hart's subcommittee, investigating the auto-insurance industry:

Mr. John R. Jewell
Commissioner Department of Motor Vehicles
Glen Burnie, Maryland

Dear Sir:

I have exhausted every course open to me, even getting an attorney as your Dealer Licensing Department suggested, and I am enclosing copies of these procedures so that you will see that a person of modest means has no recourse against a greedy and unscrupulous dealer.

As a mother of three sons under 25 and as an alarmed citizen, I am appealing to you as a person in high public office to do everything in your power to keep such cars as the "Z-28 Camaro" off public roads.

I am asking you to believe as apparently your Dealer Licensing Department would not, that I would not turn my son's driving license in for 30 days, and make him attend a second driver rehabilitation class on his own, then go out three weeks later and buy him a car with a racing rear. I give you my word that I did not know such a car existed. Also, I would ask you to believe that a 19-year-old boy would not knowingly buy a car which would use $30 worth of gas each week in driving to work when he only made $72 a week. This salesman and the owner of the company deliberately took advantage of my son's naïveté and my ignorance of the mechanics of automobiles.

I had my son's driving record with me, as I had been told by one agent that he would have trouble getting physical damage insurance as he now had liability and property damage under assigned risk. After explaining all this to the agent on the premises, this agent took our application and said there should be no problem (after viewing my son's DMV record). I asked for assurance that we would have coverage before signing the contract and the manager guaranteed the financed portion in case of collision. I have underscored this in red on the purchase order. However, this car was later in a four-car collision which was not my son's fault, after Motors Insurance Corp., had cancelled his policy and I was then told that VSI only covers the financed portion after the car is repossessed and also that a suit can be placed against you for the difference in what a car is sold for and what you owe.

One week after we had signed the contracts, Motors Insurance Corp. cancelled the insurance.

Mr. Amos of AAA Automobile Club has subsequently told me that the rate of premium for this "Z-28" with my son's points and being a teen-ager, would be in excess of $1,000 a year. This proves that Motors Insurance Corp. did not intend to insure the car in the first place, as their agent knew what kind of a car he was buying.

I did not want my son on the road with a car of this type with the racing rear end. Mr. Bestpitch, the manager of the service department at Gladding Chevro-

113

let, told me that they do not even like to sell this car to an adult because of the tremendous service problem and do not stock it. Also that a teen-age boy had no business with a car with such a fast rear. I paid to have this taken out and replaced with a conventional rear end, and he still only gets 10 miles to the gallon of gas.

The deal was fraudulent from beginning to end, as we did not get the car we signed the contract to get. The one on the purchase order had body damage which my son objected to and asked them to change it and they promised to do this. If they had given him the car he was supposed to get, at least we would not have had to replace the defective motor. We had the car back to them three times and they would not replace anything—finally when it stopped running we had to take it to Gladding.

I cannot tell you all the expense, inconvenience and heartache the purchase of this automobile has caused. From our experience with it, I urge you to try to prevent its sale in our state.

The sales pressure now seems to emphasize power and speed and I have become more conscious of it. Also, I drive the beltway to work and as I see horrible accidents and read of them in the newspaper, all seem to go hand in hand with super speed and super power.

We cannot sell or trade this car as we have too much financed—more actually than it is worth. We have become reconciled to the fact that no one will help us. But will you please do what you can to keep others from becoming the victims of this type of fraud?

The pressure that has been applied by the insurers is beginning to pay off. Ford has lowered the horsepower in some of these cars, in hopes that the insurers will lift the surcharges. General Motors, however, says it will not be lowering the horsepower of its cars this year. The company does admit that it is reducing the compression ratios to enable its cars to use lower-lead gasolines. This in effect will lower horsepower somewhat.

There is another problem in auto repairs that has been receiving national attention recently. In addition to the high labor rates charged by the body-repair and motor-repair shops, there has been a marked increase in the cost of parts. It is not unusual today to get three different estimates on body damage that vary by $100 or even $200. It all depends upon the shop and what work will be done. If a motorist insists that replacement parts be used instead of using the old parts, the cost will double or even triple in some cases. One repair shop may include the cost of head-lamp adjustment and front-end alignment, while another will not. But it is the so-called "crash parts" that are costing the most money. These are sheet-metal parts like the hood, side panels, and fenders that are replaced by the auto manufacturers. The cost of parts to assemble a 1969 Chevrolet Impala complete would be $7,500. Add to this another $7,500 in labor, and the replacement car would cost $15,000. The same car off the showroom floor would cost $3,500. Ford has agreed that the replacement-parts problem is an expensive one, and it has sharply reduced the cost of sheet-metal parts.

Insurers are leaning toward a rating system that will include factors allowing for the repairability of a car. If the consumer wants a car that is crowded with gadgets and bad design features, requiring high repairability costs, then the motorist must pay higher rates for his vehicle-damage insurance.

Many unnecessary insurance dollars are lost because of factors that neither the insurer nor the motorist have control over. The insurers can impose rating restrictions on particularly bad automobiles with high repairability costs. But the real pressure to force Detroit into building better cars will have to come from the consumers. It would not take long for manufacturers to realize that they have to build safer cars if motorists become more selective in what they purchase. If Detroit thinks it can get away with manufacturing flimsy death traps, it will.

NEGLIGENCE LAW

The negligence laws under which automobile accident cases are decided had their beginnings in the ancient Anglo-Saxon world, and until 40 or 50 years ago, these laws served us well enough. They were never conceived or meant for the motor madness of modern times. We still live with these antiquated laws—or, more often than not, suffer with them.

Negligence is defined by our courts as the failure to exercise ordinary care. It is the doing of some act which a person of reasonable prudence would not do. Negligence is also relative. This means that, in the court's judgment of negligence, the conduct of a party must be considered in view of the surrounding circumstances which are presented in evidence. An act that is negligent under one set of circumstances may not be negligent under another. An act must be proved negligent and the proximate cause of the accident before liability can be determined.

In an automobile accident, the first determination of fault is made at the scene, by police officers who may or may not issue citations. The second determination is made by the insurance company of each driver. If, in the estimation of the insurers, fault is clearly and obviously apparent, the case can be settled without a trial. The courts are the third and last step, where the issue of negligence will be settled if necessary. More often than not, it is the mere threat of court, and the forgone conclusion that a trial may be anywhere from one to five

116

years away, that prompts out-of-court settlements. If the courts had to try just one third of all accident cases, the delays might be as long as ten years. The finding of fault in a court proceeding has been described by Professor William Prosser of the University of California's Hastings College of Law as being "cumbersome, time-consuming, expensive, and almost ridiculously inaccurate. . . ." Witnesses are asked to describe in detail events that took place years before. Judges and juries are often completely overwhelmed and bewildered with conflicting testimony from participants in an accident who cannot remember what happened just prior to the collision.

When a case is brought before the court and testimony given, it must be decided who was at fault; the court must measure the evidence against what a hypothetical reasonable man would have done under the same circumstances. The court may find that all parties were guilty of negligence, which would automatically relieve the insurers of any financial responsibility. This is no isolated occurrence, for a recent Department of Transportation study showed that 25 percent of accident victims are found guilty of negligence. Some states have adopted comparative-negligence laws. In these states, a jury decides the degree of negligence of each driver, and the insurers pay accordingly. These laws, based upon the principle of "you must pay," have undergone some curious twists to accommodate the motoring public.

Society and the courts view traffic accidents in terms of driver behavior. The good driver, the driver who is morally and ethically responsible, is thought to be courteous, careful, and considerate. This driver simply does not cause accidents. It is the bad guy—the drinker, hot rodder, or other social undesirable—who causes accidents.

That this view is narrow-minded and verges on the absurd is of no consequence. It exists. True, many drinkers

117

cause accidents, but 75 percent of the motoring public drinks occasionally. It is also true that some hot rodders and thieves cause accidents, but so do the good guys.

Driving is thought of as a skill, and only bad drivers cause accidents. The facts indicate, however, that there are very few good drivers. The vast majority of drivers commit enough errors in one day to cause several accidents. In any three-year period, 80 percent of the accidents occurring will be caused by drivers with fewer than two traffic violations.

This 80 percent are the so-called *good drivers* who may never have had an accident. The good driver, moving along in congested traffic, is capable of committing up to nine driving errors in five minutes. A recent experiment in Berkeley, California, indicated that out of 394 observed autos, at three different locations, only 46 came to a full stop at stop signs. In another test in Kentucky, for each 1,000 drivers entering an intersection, an average of 310.4 made at least one driving error. Very few drivers know that they are poor drivers. Driving for many is a matter of personal pride, and the admission of poor driving skills is like a confession of physical inadequacy or mental illness.

Still, the courts decide negligence in traffic accidents as a matter of good-versus-bad driving skills, but in proving negligence there are additional factors that must be considered if we are to look at the present system as a fair and equitable way of determining fault. Factors such as the vehicle, environment, construction of roadways, safety devices and systems, and even the physical limitations of drivers must all be considered in any just determination of fault.

ACCIDENT CAUSES, NEGLIGENCE, AND THE COURTS

The motor vehicle, as Ralph Nader pointed out, can be "unsafe at any speed." The basic design of an automobile can be hazardous, in addition to its faulty equipment. Glistening hoods and chrome fittings can cause glare that will momentarily blind the driver; tinted windshields can produce limited vision; tires that the manufacturer sells stressing comfort and ride are offered at the expense of safety. Faulty brakes, loose steering wheels, and cracked or broken axles are just a few of the mechanical failures that can cause accidents.

Statistically, there are 948 precrash and crash factors in an accident, and of this total 265 can be directly attributed to the vehicle. How often do we see one of the automobile manufacturers in court defending itself against a negligence suit? How often do we find mechanics or tire manufacturers as well? In far more cases than is supposed, vehicle malfunction is the cause of an accident. A slow steering response caused by a defect in the steering apparatus can mean the difference between life and death in a crisis situation. All too often, the driver does not know that his steering is defective; he thinks it is supposed to be the way it is.

The vehicle itself can be the cause of injury to its occupants. After a vehicle collides with another vehicle or an obstruction, the occupants of the vehicle collide with the car. When the car stops, if the occupants are not restrained, they will continue moving, striking dashboards and windshields; occasionally they will be thrown from the car, causing serious if not fatal injuries. Seat belts have become standard equipment on all new cars, but few people use them, though recent court rulings have indicated that a motorist may be judged contributorily negligent if he drives without his seat belt fastened.

Air bags will be introduced as standard equipment in the 1973 model cars as a new in-car protective device.

The environment in which a vehicle travels is of the utmost importance in auto safety. The *Traffic Digest and Review* in April of 1965 said, "The absurdity of a traffic operating design where opposing guided projectiles are separated by paint stripes is obvious: this is the design we would use if our objective were to kill as many people as possible."

The design of many of our roads has been the work of chance operating between obstacles. The roadbeds on most two-lane roads are crowned, which greatly facilitates drainage and is ideally suited for accidents. An auto traveling along tends to drift to the side of the crowned road, where the road's excellent drainage has eroded most or all of the shoulder. Curves are especially treacherous, in that the vehicle is assisted by centrifugal force to drift off the crown onto the eroded shoulder, where it is easy to lose control.

Potholes, ruts, and frost heaves are bad enough, but the slickness of roads is a true menace. As anyone who has driven on ice knows, the control of a car can be expressed as a direct relationship between tires and road surface. The skid is a major cause of motor-vehicle accidents. Even our new superhighways leave a lot to be desired. The best highway design is only as good as the contractor who builds the road. Depressions and dips that allow water to accumulate and remain hours after a rainstorm are the result of poor construction and can be decidedly dangerous. How often do we find highway engineers or road-construction superintendents in court defending themselves against a charge of negligence? And there is no valid reason why they should not be prosecuted.

120

The highway engineer who designs a freeway ramp that is far too short to allow safe access has created a hazard which, in turn, will be the cause of innumerable accidents.

Safety barriers that terminate at a dangerous obstruction are another hazard for which the highway engineer is responsible. Untold injuries have been caused by this kind of hazard.

Traffic signals and signs are another problem for the motorist. Drivers who are unfamiliar with a roadway must observe the signals and signs that are frequently hidden in a maze of Kiwanis, motel, and "Welcome to Our City" signs. Recent tests have shown that it is humanly impossible for the motorist with even the best visual acuity to make the number of observations and decisions necessary in some traffic situations.

These tests also show that 50 percent of the motorists cannot estimate the speed of an oncoming car within a permissable error range of 20 percent on a two-lane roadway. Yet, most of our driving is done on two-lane roadways. Physical factors such as age, fatigue, vision defects, perception, reaction time, and deep-seated psychological traits all play a part in accident involvement. A decreased reaction time of a microsecond in an otherwise normal driver might mean the difference between life and death.

Society has provided itself with automobiles that are capable of speeds in excess of 100 miles per hour and speed limits permitted to some superhighways are 70 to 75 miles per hour. And yet we do not require that, as a condition for using these highways, a driver must have a reaction time sufficient to cope with situations occurring at those high speeds. Then, when an accident does happen and it eventually ends up in court, the driver with a slow reaction time may spend the rest of his life in poverty only because his slow reaction time is not a valid defense.

Another glaring example of the inadequacy of the fault system to determine negligence fairly is the multicar crash. The following situation has been postulated and proved with the assistance of computers. The effect is called the shock wave, and has been described by Robert Herman of the General Motors Research Laboratories by a mathematical theory of traffic flow.

Suppose car No. 1 is traveling along a highway at 65 or 70 miles per hour, and there is a long line of cars following it in the same direction—in other words, a typical highway situation. For some reason the driver of car No. 1 slows down appreciably, and then resumes his speed. The second car decelerates, but at a somewhat later time, because of the time lag. Car No. 3 decelerates at an even greater time lag, and so on down the line until perhaps car No. 14 smashes into the rear end of car No. 13 and car No. 15 into the rear of car No. 14 and so on. Who was at fault? The first 12 cars? The first car alone? The drivers of cars No. 14 and No. 15 may indeed be responsible, but they can hardly be called at fault in the sense that either one ran into the rear of the preceding car in a negligent manner. To say that drivers must maintain a safe distance between cars under today's congested traffic conditions is patently ridiculous. The number of multicrashes is significant to illustrate that the shock-wave effect happens with regularity.

In the spring of 1967, a car stopped in the right traveling lane of the New Jersey Turnpike in a dense fog. A second car moving along slowly managed to stop in time to avoid hitting the first car. A third car was not as fortunate, and neither were the 27 cars that followed. The first car drove off leaving a virtual junkyard behind him, with many injuries to the car occupants. Who was at fault? If we allow that it was the first car, how can any of the other cars prove it? The result is a legal tangle that in all probability will never be resolved.

Another factor that has received little attention is carbon monoxide. In heavily congested traffic, the buildup of carbon monoxide approaches dangerous levels, causing drivers to lose much of their efficiency. Response characteristics are especially vulnerable to high carbon monoxide levels. All of the effects of this poisonous gas are not known, and it could be far more serious than we think. The National Research Council in January, 1970, indicated correlations between increases in carbon monoxide concentrations and seeming susceptibility to auto accidents.

All of these factors—vehicle, environment, road design, road construction and repair, traffic lights and signs, and the physical limitations of the driver—present a systems complex. The interaction of all of these factors determines the cause of an accident. There is no causal factor that exhibits more importance than another, and our only conclusion can be that a certain amount of driver error is unavoidable.

The problem then becomes the investigating, collating, and presenting of these factors in a court of law. As Leon Green* has written, "Who can name all the factors involved in causing the collision? Who can know or discover or describe the conduct of the parties involved? Who in retrospect from the tangled fragments of evidence given by the participants or bystanders and those who arrived on the scene at a later time; from marks and measurements, calculations of time and speed, who is expert enough to reconstruct the fleeting scene with any assurance of accuracy?"

A recent study at Northwestern University revealed that

*L. Green, *Traffic Victims: Tort Law and Insurance* (1958).

college girls scored the highest in reconstructing the evidence of an automobile crash. How many college girls serve on juries? (Surprisingly, engineers and insurance investigators scored lower.) Even at this, the girls managed to score only 68.5 percent, and the lowest category scored only 33 percent out of a possible 100 percent. How can a determination of fault be made with the best analysis indicating a comprehension of 68.5 percent of the apparent factors involved? How many juries are made up of men and women whose comprehension might average less than 50 percent. Yet we ask these juries to decide questions of fault that will affect the victims for the remainder of their lives. What judge is wise enough to make decisions when his comprehension is no better or worse than his juries'?

Fault law is inextricably woven with moral right. You must pay for the hurt you inflict upon others because of your own negligence. If this moral right is valid, and it must be because it is the law of the land, then the deciding of questions of fault in automobile-accident cases where everyone is insured makes the law invalid. You, the negligent party, do not pay; your insurer does.

And, too, under the present system, there are many times when the insurer does not have to pay at all. The following case history illustrates this:

Jerry Isola left Houghton, Michigan, at 9 P.M. He was feeling very happy as this night he had passed the test of meeting his girl's parents for the first time. Not only had he felt accepted, but he genuinely liked the older couple. Jerry took the shore road from Houghton rather than the main road to Laurium, as he wanted to prolong the evening for a few moments before reaching home and studying for finals.

In the distance he thought he saw a moving light off to the side of the road. The oncoming traffic was heavy, and the lead car's high beams shone directly into Jerry's eyes. He quickly decided not to take any chances; he lifted his foot from the accelerator and started to apply the brakes when he smashed into the rear end of an unlighted parked car. Jerry was rushed to the hospital in critical condition. He was found to have suffered a crushed right chest, with fractured pleural cavity, fractured ribs, and fractured patella (knee cap). After the crash all Jerry could remember was the parked car suddenly before him and then the horrifying crash.

Investigators later proved that the driver of the parked car, after running out of gas, had shut off his lights in order to save his battery, and had stood off to the side of the road waving a flashlight.

Jerry spent the entire summer in a cast and on his first day back at Michigan Tech in the fall semester, he was still weak. During the summer Jerry's father went on strike against the C&H Mining Company, and the final payment on the medical expenses came to $3,350, which was all Mr. Isola had been able to save in 20 years of working in the C&H copper mines. Jerry had two sisters and two brothers. Each of the children pitched in to help their father, getting jobs and working full-time all summer. The youngest, a nine-year-old, even delivered papers. Mr. Isola felt confident that they would be paid by the insurance company.

In October the case finally came to trial, and the verdict was quick and merciless: contributory negligence on the part of Jerry. The court ruled that Jerry should have seen the car and should have been able to stop. The court also admonished the driver of the parked car for his contributory negligence in not leaving his lights on while he was parked. Because both drivers were guilty of contributory negligence, neither could collect from the other's insurance company. The result of this finding by the court was not simply a loss of over $3,300, but that Jerry was forced into giving up his scholarship and going to work to help support his family. The money would have been enough to see Mr. Isola's family through the winter, or at least carry them until the strike was over. The C&H strike is now going its third year, and Jerry has all but given up hope of ever being able to return to college.

Jerry's case is typical of many. The complete and utter failure of the entire insurance system to compensate accident victims for even their net medical and wage losses is deplorable and morally indefensible. In 1971, there will be over 5 million traffic accidents causing bodily injury. A goodly percentage of these will not know they have lost all they owned until their cases come to trial. Does it not seem strange that, while the insurers are debating whether $1 billion or $1.3 billion is an adequate profit, thousands of accident victims will receive no accident compensation at all?

Under the present system the average driver carries 10/20/5. That is, $10,000 insurance for injury to any one person in an accident, $20,000 limits for injuries in any one accident, and $5,000 property damage. This amount is woefully inadequate today. If our average driver were to have an accident in which he was found to be at fault, and the other vehicle contained five injured persons, his maximum coverage would probably be inadequate. If, for instance, the total economic loss value was $25,000, the guilty driver would be liable for $5,000. In addition, the jury could award an amount of $75,000 pain-and-suffering damages. This would place a financial burden of $80,000 on the average driver. Allowing him a payment of $100 per week, it would take over 15 years to pay the judgment. Every automobile owner should carry a bare minimum of $25/50/10. Coverage of $100/300/20 is a far safer amount.

Delay between accident and settlement may take as long as five years in some urban areas. The present average delay is 19 months for all accidents, involving claims above $2,500. The more serious the accident, the longer the delay. Delay causes many costly hardships to claimants, the most significant being medical and wage losses. A two-week stay in a hospital could cost as much as $1,000, not including a physician's services. Most hospitalization plans do not cover the entire cost. Loss of wages for just one month can be a financial disaster for many families. These expenses create an urge to settle with an insurer, and if the loss is under $1,500, the insurer will usually settle within a reasonable length of time. It is only the victims with serious injuries who are forced to wait for long periods of time. These victims are offered settlements far below their actual or anticipated losses. The insurers hope that financial pressures will force the claimants to accept their offers.

On a national average, only 13 percent of total loss is collected by 76 percent of the seriously injured. It is obvious that the minor claims are being satisfied quickly enough and at 200 or 300 percent over actual loss by the insurers—at the expense of the seriously injured.

Another consequence of delay is the postponement of rehabilitation. Quite often this delay results in medical problems of major proportions. Victims with loss of function in their arms or legs, for instance, respond very well to early rehabilitation procedures, and the regaining of complete function is not uncommon. Yet, for most victims, rehabilitation must wait for an insurance settlement. The delay is frequently long enough to minimize the effects of rehabilitation, and the victim may never recover the use of an arm or a leg.

Disfigurement requires immediate surgery to be effective. All too often there is no money available to pay for the multiple graftings and other surgical procedures necessary. The victims must wait for an unsympathetic insurance company that couldn't care less about the victim's condition. One of the most horrible of practices is urged on their client accident victims by some attorneys. In order that a victim may receive the largest possible settlement, he is advised to delay any medical rehabilitation, if rehabilitation or cosmetic surgery would mean that the victim would not be able to limp or crawl or present a horribly scarred countenance to the jury. It is not of the slightest concern to these attorneys that the victim may never walk again or that his face will remain scarred for life. All these attorneys are interested in is the largest percentage of the settlement they will receive as their fee, and the poor dolts who listen to this advice probably do not realize the consequences of their decisions.

Most of us can afford to withstand a mild financial disaster, even if it takes a year or two to recover. There are very few of us who can withstand a prolonged financial drain on our resources. We buy insurance, therefore, in the belief that it will help us avoid financial loss. Most of us believe that the law is just and the insurers will live up to their obligations. We see here that all of the evidence points to the contrary.

Allowing for the inadequacies of the law for a moment, what sort of inhumanity does the insurer practice? Some 99 percent of accident cases are settled out of court, the settlement procedure based upon the same determinations that the courts would have used had they tried the cases. There is nothing in any auto-insurance policy that states that the insurer will decide questions of law; however, settlements are based upon the evidence collected by the adjuster.

The Northwestern study showed that the trained investigator was not as good as the college girl in evidence comprehension, yet this man decides who will be paid and how much he will be paid, according to company rules. It is not unheard of that an adjuster will offer a fast settlement at the hospital bedside of a half-alive victim for one hundreth of a fair settlement. A victim coming out of shock and groggy from the effects of sedatives or other medication is not too difficult a subject for the adjuster.

Why do we allow an insurance company to decide who will eat, who will walk, or who will be able to care for his children? Did we not purchase insurance to protect us from these disasters? Since when have we allowed our life styles to be dictated by the whims of the insurers? The very least an insurer could provide is a degree of humanity.

Morality alone dictates that the current practice of claims reparation be reversed. Badly injured victims should be compensated for their injuries and their wage losses as they accrue. If anyone can afford to wait, those with minor losses can, but even these should be dealt with justly.

PAIN AND SUFFERING

"Pain and suffering" or "general damages" are terms used in accident reparations. The theory behind pain and suffering is that an accident victim should be paid for his intangible losses. These might be mental anguish, physical disabilities, loss of future income, or just an outright gift. There are no rules as to how an amount of money can justly compensate an accident victim for his injuries beyond his actual economic loss. How do you put a price on the loss of a limb, paraplegia, or a scratch on the forehead? Yet juries and insurance companies have been trying to do this for years. The theory has been replaced with the fact that pain and suffering awards are merely bargaining tools. Many people regard it as the attorney's fee.

I. M. Cohen was involved in an automobile accident four years ago in upper New York State. The accident was clearly not his fault, and the defendant, the one at fault, was a wealthy man. Mr. Cohen had been employed as an accountant for 12 years and earned $12,000 per year. He was married and had two children in junior high school.

Mr. Cohen had both arms broken, and severe facial lacerations with permanent loss of sight in both eyes. His total medical expenses came to $11,000. His wage loss in the four years he was out of work amounted to $36,580 after consideration for taxes. If Mr. Cohen had worked his normal work life, he would have had another 18 years of earnings ahead of him. Without any consideration for wage increases, his future loss of income after taxes amounted to $164,110. Mr. Cohen's attorney put in a claim of $500,000 in order to insulate the claim against possible dilution through bargaining with the insurer, calling it pain and suffering.

The insurer offered $75,000 prior to the trial and another offer of $95,000 on the courthouse steps. The defendant had liability coverage of $100,000 and $300,000. If the man at fault received a judgment exceeding these limits, he would be personally responsible for the excess amount.

The trial lasted four days, and Mr. Cohen received $47,580 for his actual loss, and the jury was given the chore of deciding the amount to be awarded as pain and suffering. The jury awarded $25,000. Why the jury offered such an insignificant amount is debatable. Perhaps they felt sorry for the defendant, who had appeared on the stand as shabbily dressed as any derelict from the Bowery. Perhaps they were biased because Mr. Cohen spoke well and despite his blindness carried himself with dignity. Whatever the reason, the award stood, with no change possible.

130

Mr. Cohen received a total of $72,580, and his lawyer's fee came to just over $18,000. The attorney was deeply disturbed by the outcome of the case and absorbed the $4,000 in expenses he had incurred in preparing the case. The net amount Mr. Cohen received was $54,580. From this amount he still had to deduct medical expenses and money he had borrowed. Mrs. Cohen had to go to work, and with the small amount of money remaining, Mr. Cohen is undergoing extensive rehabilitation. At best, he and his family can expect to exist on a marginal basis for many years.

Mr. Cohen was fortunate in the sense that he collected at all. Many hundreds of thousands of victims have not collected one cent. Would it not have been better if Mr. Cohen had received compensation according to his needs and for as long as the need existed? The large-claims settlements are few and the suits brought against the insurers are usually headlines in the newspapers; however, the actual settlements seldom make the news at all. The fact here is that Mr. Cohen was entitled to receive at least $211,690 ($36,580 lost wages plus $11,000 medical expense, plus $164,110 future wage loss); that is the minimum he would have earned, plus his wage loss and medical expenses to the date of the trial.

In a minor claim, $1,000 or less, insurance companies think little of paying the victim two or three times his loss. As a result there are many thousands of minor-accident victims who think the present system is wonderful. When a minor scratch, a three-day vacation from work, and a vague complaint of pain somewhere in the lower back can get a victim $800 or $900, he will be against any change in a system that allows such generosity. If one of these claimants had a serious accident, he would find the insurance companies significantly less generous.

Slightly less than $1.3 billion was paid out by the

131

insurance companies in 1970 for pain and suffering. This outlay will increase by another $250 million in 1971. A recent Department of Transportation study revealed that claimants with a permanent disability had an average total economic loss of $78,000, yet they received only an average of $12,556, 16 percent of their economic loss. Certainly the seriously injured are not receiving any substantial part of the $1.3 billion in pain and suffering that has been paid out by the insurers.

Another aspect of pain-and-suffering awards, and of any settlements paid in a lump sum, is that most people are not used to handling large sums of money. When an award or settlement is paid to the victim, he too frequently spends it on a new car, furniture, and vacation, and the like. Seldom is there any thought given to the future medical expenses and wage losses that the victim will experience because of his disability. Many times the money is spent, and the victims become welfare cases.

Periodic payments, at intervals of a month or every three months, would save the victims from their own extravagance.

The present auto-insurance system has concerned itself primarily with indemnification of loss and has paid little attention to the problems of accident prevention. A change in the present system would allow a wealth of information regarding accident causes to become useful in accident prevention. Information concerning vehicles, environment, road design, and driver traits could be available for statistical analysis, allowing us to predict accurately the causes and to provide solutions toward accident prevention.

If, for instance, the auto manufacturers were told that the incidence of metal fatigue in axles on all models of a certain year were causing an alarming number of accidents, the manufacturers could recall these vehicles, or at least issue warnings to owners regarding the problem. If the manufacturers failed to take immediate action, the insurers could refuse to insure those models until corrective measures were taken.

If the insurers were to find out that a certain type of highway construction was conducive to accidents, they could inform the agency in charge of roads about the situation. The issue, if need be, could be forced in several ways. For example, signs could be erected warning motorists of a particular hazard as an interim measure while a court action against the state for the elimination of the hazard was being instituted.

If a preponderance of evidence indicated that certain physical traits were a principal factor in accident causation, licensing authorities could be apprised of these factors and appropriate action taken. To force the issue these drivers could be refused insurance.

THE PROBLEM WITH ALCOHOL

It is no secret that drinking drivers are a serious problem. For years we have watched the mounting toll of deaths and injuries caused by these drivers. The solution to the problem has been to create slogans, form discussion groups, and impose penalties on the offenders. What we have done is treat the effects and not the causes of the problem. Threats of penalties are largely ignored. Every person who drinks and drives is aware of his potential for harm. At any given time 10 percent of the drivers on our nation's roads have been drinking. Obviously the solution has not worked.

The drunken driving of the alcoholic is not a deliberate action, but the effect of physical and mental conditions; it is a disease. What is needed is a comprehensive program of

133

assistance with psychiatric help, restricted driving hours, special license plates for identification purposes, and perhaps even voluntary medication. The drug antabuse, for example, causes a violent reaction to alcohol. Daily dosages are required and could be given by local pharmacies to alcoholics who requested the drug.

The social drinker, however, presents other problems; he is largely responsible for his actions. It is difficult for the social drinker to estimate his loss of function after one or two drinks; his mental high seems to override his capacity. As a consequence the driver who has had a couple of drinks loses valuable degrees of response and perception which frequently leads to an accident. The social drinker is certainly aware that he should not drink and drive, but he undoubtedly feels that he will not have an accident. Nor does he want to be arrested for his drinking.

This fact has been borne out in England. The accident rate due to driving under the influence of alcohol was sharply reduced in that country when police officers were allowed to use an alcohol detection device on drivers at will.

Licensing authorities in the States have never faced the problem of drinking drivers squarely. The insurers, however, have the resources to meet this problem and to force appropriate agencies of government to take corrective action. The mere surcharging of any motorist who has a history of a drinking problem, unless he could completely satisfy the insurer that he would not drive under the influence of alcohol, would be a start. This would require investigation beyond the perusal of driving records, and undoubtedly would be disagreeable to many people. The drinking-driver problem, however, is of such magnitude that drastic measures are necessary to control it.

One final note on drunken driving. The fact that a driver has been drinking while driving does not necessarily mean that he would be liable under the negligence law. The plaintiff must prove that the influence of alcohol was the proximate cause of the accident. Too, the defendant drinking driver can free himself from liability if he can prove contributory negligence on the part of the plaintiff.

Drugged driving has also become a problem. At this time, there is no reliable evidence to indicate just how serious the problem might be. Police officers in some states are being trained in drug-detection procedures. At best these are merely pilot programs, and it will be some time before their effectiveness is realized.

MERIT PLANS

The merit driving plans in use today are unfair, discriminatory, and expensive for the motorists. A typical merit plan is based upon a driver's past performance. The number of traffic violations and accidents he has or does not have determines his surcharge or discount of premium.

In the Commonwealth of Massachusetts, a recently enacted law requires that the surcharge be based upon each conviction of a moving violation committed by the owner, any member of his household, or any other person authorized to drive the policyholder's vehicle. The surcharge schedule allows, for each conviction of driving under the influence of intoxicating liquors or narcotics or hallucinogenic drugs, a surcharge of 100 percent, for each conviction of speeding, a surcharge of 20 percent, for each conviction of any other moving violation, a surcharge of 10 percent. No one surcharge would be in effect for longer than five years. The discount schedule allows for a discount of 2 percent for each full year free of accident involvement up to a maximum of 10 percent.

In many states, merit plans call for surcharges because

of accidents. A motorist sustaining a $65 dent in his fender might have to pay a surcharge of over $300 per year for three years, because of the merit system. Practices of this sort are decidedly wrong and should be eliminated.

Merit plans, in these instances, are being used to intimidate motorists. What driver in his right mind is going to report an accident in which he only sustained $75 in damages, knowing that it is going to cost him $900? The merit plan can be a useful tool to discourage improper and illegal driving practices, and it should be restricted to that end.

THE NEW YORK NO-FAULT PLAN

We have seen what the present system of auto insurance, with its callous indifference to the plight of the insured, is and what it is costing us. Our courts have become a farce, dispensing inhumanity and injustice with a swing of the gavel and with the consent of biased juries. It would be simple to recant this sad litany of offenses forever, but it is now time for solutions. The complete overhaul of the present insurance system is within our capabilities, but first we must know the quality of the system we hope to replace it with, and what it will cost us.

The New York Insurance Department is recognized as the leading force for progressive and effective insurance regulation in the country. In more recent years, the department has been in the vanguard of those interested in automobile-insurance reform. As might be expected, the New York No-Fault Plan is a model for effective reform, characterized by a comprehensive and meaningful reparations system. This plan is significant in that it provides unlimited no-fault benefits. Any system of reform has to be fundamental in design and revolutionizing in its effects. Systems that answer only part of the problem meet only part of the consumers' needs.

Before we go into the details of the New York plan, there is one thought we must consider. This plan is only a legislative skeleton, to which must be added additional features and procedures upon its adoption. The task of streamlining and molding the final legislated plan is a task for the insurers, the state insurance department, and any interested citizen who can contribute sound and valuable ideas for a fair and responsible auto-insurance system.

There have been many detractors of the New York plan who have not understood the nature of the plan, and who do not understand the procedures of implementing legislation. This does not mean that this plan or any other submitted by a government agency is beyond reproach and should not be questioned. Indeed, debate and strong responsible opposition are needed and are welcomed. The thought here is that the debate and the opposition should concern themselves with real issues and not fringe anomalies.

The New York Plan, as submitted to Governor Rockefeller by the state insurance department, contains specific recommendations. These are as follows:

1. Reparations would be made on a no-fault basis.
2. Private enterprise should operate the plan.
3. Complete medical coverage should be provided.
4. Unlimited wage benefits should be offered.
5. Auto insurance should be compulsory.
6. There should be no duplication of benefits.
7. There should be no allowance for pain and suffering.
8. The system should be reliable.
9. Other categories.

Reparation would be made on a no-fault basis. No-fault means just what its name implies—that negligence suits based on the operation of motor vehicles would be abolished. The adversary system would be replaced with a

140

direct claims-making action against the claimant's own insurer. For example, in two-car accidents, neither car owner would recover from the other for automobile damage or bodily injury. Each driver's insurance company would settle with its own insured driver, except in the case of death, where the New York constitution permits no change in the recovery of damages.

Many critics of no-fault have contended that such a system would not be constitutional, because it impairs a citizen's right to due process and equal protection under the Fifth and Fourteenth Amendments of the Constitution of the United States. Professor Lindsey Cowan, dean of the University of Georgia Law School, states the problem as follows:

> The Constitutional questions are said to arise because these provisions (of no-fault) arbitrarily limit or reduce the existing rights of some and expand the existing obligations of others. Such reduction, it has been said, constitutes a denial of due process or equal protection with respect to an individual who, under traditional tests, is in no way at fault for his own injuries received in an automobile accident, but who is forced under the plan to accept less compensation than that to which under the common law he would have been entitled from one at fault. Similarly, it is claimed, the expansion of responsibility may be a denial of due process or equal protection with respect to an individual who is not at fault, yet who must pay through the medium of insurance not only for his own injuries, but also for those of others who themselves may or may not have been at fault.

Professor Cowen is a noted authority on constitutional law, and he has investigated the issue in great detail in

141

a study entitled "Due Process, Equal Protection and No-Fault Allocation of the Costs of Automobile Accidents."*

The professor concluded his study with the following summary:

"Nevertheless, on the basis of such information as is available, it seems reasonable to predict that for the foreseeable future, at least, the no-fault plans for the allocation of the costs of automobile accidents do not violate the due process and equal protection clauses of the Fourteenth Amendment."

Professor Joseph W. Bishop, Jr., of Yale University Law School, writing in the same publication,* rendered the opinion that adoption of no-fault plans would not be declared unconstitutional in any of the states.

Many of the arguments regarding the constitutionality of no-fault are based upon workmen's compensation laws. All states have these laws, and these laws provide that compensation will be paid to workers injured on the job, regardless of fault and without an adversary proceeding.

We can assume that the New York No-Fault Plan will not be declared unconstitutional at either the state or federal level. An accident victim will be relieved of all the doubt and anxiety of court decisions, and he will be in a much better situation for dealing directly with his own insurer.

Private Enterprise Could Operate the Plan. The New York plan specifically relies upon the present insurance establishment to operate the no-fault plan. There are two government study groups that have been conducting

*This study was published in *Constitutional Problems in Automobile Accident Compensation Reform,* which was financed and published by the U.S. Department of Transportation as part of its investigation of the auto-insurance industry.

142

extensive investigations into auto-insurance problems. Senator Hart, of the Senate Subcommittee on Antitrust and Monopoly, has already submitted a no-fault plan as a result of his committee's investigation. We will examine this plan later in this section.

The Department of Transportation concluded a two-year investigation of the auto insurance industry, and the final report was released in April of 1971. The report summarized the most comprehensive study ever undertaken of the automobile insurance system. The report also advocated a no-fault approach as being the most efficacious and humane answer to the present reparations system.

Political pressures (some say from the White House), however, caused the Secretary of Transportation, Mr. Volpe, not to press for a Federal No-Fault Bill. What Mr. Volpe is advocating is that each state decide for itself whether or not to adopt a no-fault plan.

The present insurance establishment in New York State has the resources and is capable of operating a no-fault plan within the state. Indeed, it is probable that insurers can operate a no-fault plan in every state.

Complete Medical Coverage Would Be Provided. The plan would provide complete medical services, such as hospital, physician, specialist, surgeon, nursing, and home-nursing care. All of these expenses would be completely paid for in the event of injuries sustained in an automobile accident. If, for instance, an accident victim had injuries that would confine him to a hospital for many years, the plan would pay all medical expenses, including posthospital care, and for as long as the victim required them.

All reasonable physical and occupational therapy would be provided. This means that, if an accident victim lost a limb, the plan would provide rehabilitation services, including the supply of a prosthetic device. The victim

143

could then be trained in an occupation, if possible, that he could perform with his disability.

Under the medical services provision of the plan, the victim would be paid for any services that he normally would have performed but, for reason of the accident, is unable to perform. These would include baby-sitting, house cleaning, taxi service, etc. All medical bills would be paid by the insurer as they accrued.

Unlimited Wage Loss Benefits Would Be Provided. The provision allowing for unlimited wage-loss benefits is of considerable importance. Accident victims would be paid all wages normally due them through the entire course of their recovery, or if the victim was disabled for life, he would receive his wages as he normally would have had he been able to work. Payments would be made periodically, perhaps weekly or monthly.

Auto Insurance Would Be Compulsory and Would Cost Less. All motorists within the State of New York would be required to purchase auto insurance. Because of the nature of first-party no-fault plans, every motorist is compensated by his own insurer and has no recourse to litigation. Therefore, every motorist would have to be insured.

Auto insurance would cost less under the plan. All accident cases could be processed as a matter of form rather than relying on case-by-case determinations of fault. This would enable the insurers to standardize the procedures which, in turn, would lend themselves to automation. There are no figures available to project any definite savings through the elimination of court action, though there may be some cases where some court findings might be necessary, a savings of 75 percent in attorneys' fees is not too unrealistic a goal. The elimination of pain-and-suffering awards would amount to more savings.

144

The plan, however, is expected to provide benefits for a much larger number of claimants than the present system allows. The savings incurred through the reductions and elimination of the above items would be more than enough to offset this additional cost. In fact, the New York plan is predicted to save in the vicinity of one third or more over present rates.

The plan pays unlimited wage benefits, regardless of wages earned. Accordingly, the rates will have to be based upon the amount of wages a motorist earns. These will be net wages, exclusive of federal, state, and municipal taxes. Thus, the motorist earning $1,000 per month will pay more for his auto insurance than the motorist earning only $500 per month. All other benefits would be the same for all motorists regardless of wage level.

There Would Be No Duplication of Benefits. Under the New York plan, there would be no duplication of benefits. Auto insurance would be secondary to other collateral benefits. For instance, if an accident victim were covered by Blue Cross, Blue Shield, and some form of wage-continuation insurance, he would have to use these benefits to their limits before his auto-insurance company would pay any benefits. Those motorists not covered by collateral insurance would be compensated fully by the auto insurer.

In order to internalize motoring costs, Blue Cross and similar insurers should be prohibited from allowing motorists to collect at all under their policies for auto-accident injuries. All of the collateral insurers could then reduce their rates with this understanding, and the cost of their insurance would be decreased.

Blue Cross, for instance, filed for a 19.3 percent increase in December of 1970 in New York. If it did not have the responsibility for paying a motorist's injuries, this increase might not have been necessary. There is no valid reason why the general public, in any way, should have to bear the cost of the motoring public. There is no valid reason under the present system why motorists should not pay higher premiums under their auto insurance for this medical coverage.

One problem with some motorists whose employers offer sick-pay benefits is that these benefits could be used up in a minor accident. The employer would then have to pay for the employee's loss of wages up to the limits of company policy. Later in that same year, should the employee get sick, he would have no benefits left. The solution is that all employers would have to exclude auto accidents as a compensable wage benefit.

There Would Be No Allowance for Pain and Suffering. Pain and suffering or general damages would not be paid under the compulsory-insurance plan. This means that victims could not collect for more than their actual loss. In the case of dismemberment or disfigurement, the victim would be given every medical assistance possible, and his wages would be paid by the insurer. He would not, however, be paid anything more than that. Regardless of whether he was involved in a hit-and-run accident, an accident with a drunken driver, or was simply walking down the street and hit by a car, the victim would not recover more than his economic loss.

The innocent victim destined to suffer a lifetime of horrible disfigurement or dismemberment, because of the wanton and irresponsible action of a motorist, may feel hatred and desire revenge, and he would especially want the guilty motorist to pay severely for his crime. These feelings are normal and above all understandable. But even under the present system of auto insurance the guilty party does not pay; his insurer pays. If a negligent driver's actions were criminal, he would be tried under other than insurance laws for his crime. What is more, statistics show that the majority of the seriously injured victims under the present system do not receive their net economic loss, not to mention any payment for their pain and suffering. Once more, evidence also indicates that fault is the result of many factors and, except for the case of the drunken driver, is very difficult to prove.

It is much more humane to have a system which will pay for all of the losses a victim might suffer without any limitations. There are a few isolated instances where an auto-accident victim receives a substantial award for his pain and suffering or general damages, but these are very few. The bulk of this money is paid to victims with minor claims, who in turn hand much of it over to their attorneys.

The New York plan has made some provision for the payment of cash benefits to motorists who sustain physical impairments. The benefits would be paid on an objective basis similar to payments made under workmen's compensation for physical impairment. This coverage would be available on an optional basis and would involve additional cost to the policyholder.

The System Would Be Reliable. The New York plan would be reliable in that policyholders would know exactly what benefits would be theirs in the event of an accident, and they would have recourse if payments were not made on time by the insurers. There would be little reason for the insurers to delay, but if they did for no valid reason, the state insurance department would impose heavy sanctions and fines on the offenders.

This plan, proposed by the New York Insurance Department, eliminates many of the delays that occur

147

naturally under the present system. The case-by-case determination, as it is now done, is slow, expensive, and cumbersome. The new no-fault plan offers a system eliminating these individual determinations. All cases would be handled in the same manner, which would greatly facilitate computerized operations, and would allow the flexibility necessary for the heavy caseloads of the future.

The most important aspect of the new system's reliability is the insurer's capability of furnishing benefits far into the future. In some instances, insurers will be required to make periodic payments for totally disabled victims for many years. Part of this responsibility will fall upon the state insurance departments. They will have to be more careful than ever before that each insurer maintains safe claim reserves. To this end, the state has recently begun an extensive analysis of insolvencies and of solvency requirements. Other states will surely follow New York's lead.

Other Aspects of the Plan. A merit driving program could be part of the plan. Under the merit program, accident-free motorists are allowed discounts, and lawbreakers are assessed points for each violation, which in turn will be factors in their rates. Certain obnoxious categories of drivers would be severely penalized through the merit program. Drunken, drugged, and other socially abhorrent drivers would have to pay a surcharge as a percentage of premium for a violation, and this surcharge would be in force for a specified number of years.

Under the program, every motorist is responsible for damages to his own car. Collision insurance would be available on the same first-party basis as it is available now. Motorists, however, would not be liable for damages to another vehicle, but only to other property for which property-damage insurance would be available.

The owners of commercial vehicles would have the same responsibilities as the owners of private passenger cars, plus one additional responsibility: they would be liable for damage to a private passenger car, or injury to its occupants. While the private-vehicle owner would recover normally through his insurance company, the insurer would have a claim against the commercial vehicle owner, or his insurer, but only for the amount that the private-car insurer had paid out in benefits. The rationale here is that commercial vehicle owners can better distribute their accident costs than can the owner of a private passenger car. The commercial vehicle owner can also: influence driving conduct through the hiring of expert drivers, elect to purchase only those vehicles which are proven safe, and purchase only those vehicles with low repairability features. Automobile manufacturers are far more inclined to listen and to remedy the problems and complaints of a customer who purchases five or six thousand taxicabs a year as opposed to the one- or two-vehicle private buyer.

ARGUMENTS AGAINST
THE NEW YORK PLAN

The foes of no-fault constitute a most formidable opposition. Composed mainly of trial lawyers and the majority of the insurers, these foes have resorted to a number of strategies to denounce the plan. This royal opposition dictates its wishes to the state legislatures, as the following editorial in the *Albany Times Union* of May 17, 1970, illustrates:

> Yet the system is perpetuated, reform is rejected year after year for only one major reason: the legislature is really part of the insurance establishment.

149

Its members are mostly attorneys. Large numbers of attorneys derive large amounts of income from handling auto accident insurance cases. The proposed reforms would eliminate much of this income. Thus the legislators have a vested interest in the status quo; it may be in the public interest to reform our auto insurance structure, but that doesn't seem to count. What does seem to count mostly is that they take advantage of existing law to charge outrageous rates for poor service to the public. The service is promoted by the legal fraternity which gets a quarter to a third or even more of all the many millions of dollars worth of settlements or jury awards.

Then, in another editorial on May 20, 1970, the Albany *Times Union* said:

The reform bill sponsored by Governor Rockefeller has so far been kept bottled up in committee by the legislative leadership, which is under extreme pressure from the state and local bar associations and the insurance lobby to prevent any significant changes in the present system.

This problem is not confined to New York. In every state where no-fault plans have been introduced, the trial-lawyers associations and others have mounted fierce and incisive attacks to defeat them. In Massachusetts their efforts have not been quite as successful as they might have wished. The legislators in that state passed a modified no-fault plan that hardly deserves to be called a no-fault plan at all, due to its watered-down provisions.

These attorneys have banded together and are showing a united front in their opposition to no-fault. Their arguments against the plan center on the principle that it is not right to take away the common-law rights of the people, nor is it right to destroy the concept of liability for the person at fault. Further, they claim that fault liability is an effective deterrent to bad driving.

As we have repeatedly shown in previous chapters, common law is an archaic, inhumane, and arbitrary method of determining automobile-accident cases. Dean William Prosser, of the University of California's Hastings College of Law, comments on the trial of auto negligence cases as follows:

> The process by which the question of legal fault, and hence of liability (in automobile accident cases) as determined in our courts is cumbersome, time-consuming, expensive and almost ridiculously inaccurate. The evidence given in personal injury cases usually consists of highly contradictory statements from the two sides, estimating such factors as time, speed, distance, and visibility, offered months after the event by witnesses who were never very sure just what happened when they saw it, and whose faulty memories are undermined by lapse of time, by bias, by conversations with others, and by the subtle influence of counsel. Upon such evidence, a jury of 12 inexperienced citizens, called away from their other business, if they have any, are invited to retire and make the best guess they can as to whether the defendant, the plaintiff, or both were negligent, which is itself a wobbly and uncertain standard based upon the supposed mental process of a hypothetical and non-existent, reasonable man. European lawyers view the whole thing with utter amazement; and the extent to which it has damaged the courts and the legal profession by bringing the law and its administration into public disrepute can only be guessed.

The practice of law is an honored profession and one held in high esteem by most people. There are lawyers, however, who are not as honorable and honest as they could be, and there are lawyers who are downright dishonest. It is the ambulance chaser, the courtroom actor, who brings the profession into disrepute. Now we have an issue that is so clearly obvious, an issue wherein the law no longer serves the purpose for which it was intended, that even legal scholars are calling for change. Of course the primary issue here is money. Some authorities believe that auto-accident fees constitute half of all trial lawyers' incomes per year. The abolition of the fault principle would cost the trial lawyers about 50 percent of their income. It is not our purpose to dictate lifestyles for anyone, but it would seem that lawyers' incomes should not be at the expense of policyholders and claimants.

The insurers, too, have been marshaling their forces and are sniping and pecking at the no-fault plans. New York's plan has come under a particularly vicious attack by the American Mutual Insurance Alliance and various insurance agents' associations. What is amusing about their attacks is that they would tear apart the no-fault plan for some of the same reasons that we find the present system so abhorrent. There is one argument that bears repeating verbatim. Donald W. Segraves, vice-president, American Mutual Insurance Alliance, writing in *Trial* magazine, in the October-November issue of 1970 said:

> Higher rates would be required for the following categories of people under the Governor's proposed first-party system. . . . Persons living in areas subject to high accident frequency, because of traffic congestion, poor weather conditions, inadequate law enforcement, or other environmental factors. This includes older sections of major cities.
>
> Persons likely to incur more expensive medical treatment in the event of a disabling injury. [This factor is most bewildering.]

152

Persons prone to hazardous driving behavior, including abusive use of alcohol, and drugs, speeding and other aggressive or reckless forms of driving. Young drivers, for example, tend to have more frequent and more severe accidents because of the way they drive.

Persons exhibiting more "claims consciousness" than the general population. . . .

The pomposity of these charges is overwhelming. It is as if the insurers had no rating classifications at all. What does Mr. Segraves call the premium for the under-25 driver, at present higher than what the average driver pays by more than 100 percent? The insurers today will seldom insure ghetto residents, and here is the statement that they will have to pay more under the governor's plan. This sort of argument is blatantly irresponsible, coming from the vice-president of a major insurance organization.

Some insurers also claim that no-fault will cost the motorist more than the present system. We disagree with this statement most heartily. The actuaries in the employ of the insurance companies are certainly no better than those working for the New York State Insurance Department. In fact, there are several actuaries in the department whose stature is recognized across the country as being the very best available.

The elimination of costly litigation, pain and suffering, duplication of benefits, and the opportunity for the insurers to automate their procedures fully under the new plan make the predictions of 33 percent rate reductions conservative. Too, why did the insurers in Massachusetts agree to a 15 percent reduction in bodily-injury rates when the state adopted a modified no-fault plan if they did not feel that the plan would save on insurance costs? They certainly reacted over the rate decreases in property damages and comprehensive insurance, and went to the Supreme Court of that state to have them rescinded. It

153

would appear that some insurers are merely using scare tactics to fight the no-fault concept.

Also, there is the argument that a no-fault system would require additional rating classifications. The insurers presently have a so-called 260 plan, which allows over 100,000 different rates in a large state. The system is patently ridiculous in the face of statistics. As we explained earlier, in any three-year period, 80 percent of accidents will be caused by the good risks. Further, in order to reduce the number of accidents appreciably in any one year, 50 percent of the motorists would have to be taken from the roads. It would appear that the insurers have become victims of their own system. We are not disputing that there is a hazardous group of drivers who have identifiable characteristics. We are not disputing that there should not be separate and higher rates for this class of driver. What we do feel is wrong is that the insurers have lost control of their objectives through the oversophistication of the means to their objective.

What is really at stake with the insurers is resistance to change. This is understandable. It will not be until states like New York, Minnesota, and a few others have passed a comprehensive no-fault plan into law and the insurers are forced to comply with its provisions that this resistance will end. Then they will see that the system is workable, will save the policyholders money, and will allow the insurers to face the future with a plan that will be readily adaptable to its needs.

The superintendent of the New York Insurance Department, Richard E. Stewart, offered an evaluation of his department's plan:

> There are no perfect plans. Around the edges of any new system it will always be possible to conjure anomalous situations and strange results, but that is

due to the complexity of the problem and should not be cause for despair. Nor should it be an excuse for endless disputation about fringe anomalies while the fault insurance system, anomalous to the core, remains unchanged.

The best we can do is decide upon the criteria for a good system and then, when inevitable choices among criteria have to be made, to make the choices according to sensible priorities. If we can do that much, we will have done a lot and we will have done all we can do. It will then be time to act.

BASIC PROTECTION

Any discussion of no-fault insurance would not be complete without mentioning the contributions of the men who really gave the concept life in this country. They are Professors Robert E. Keeton, Harvard Law School, and Jeffrey O'Connell, University of Illinois. Their book, *Basic Protection for the Traffic Victim*, published in 1965, was the ingredient necessary to stimulate auto-insurance reform. Several of the main provisions of their plan are as follows:

1. Partial replacement of negligence liability insuance with no-fault insurance. Ten thousand dollar limit on no-fault with a deduction of $5,000 on pain and suffering. Any claims for more than these amounts would require a normal tort recovery procedure.

2. Benefits would be paid as losses accrued on a month-to-month basis, and limited to net economic loss. Collateral or duplicate benefits would be subtracted from amounts paid, including wage-loss insurance and sick pay.

3. The original Basic Protection Plan did not include property damage; a more recent version does.

4. Basic protection would be compulsory on all automobiles registered in every state adopting the plan.

5. Rehabilitation and occupational therapy would be provided.

6. Present tort procedures would be preserved for settling disputed claims.

The Basic Protection Plan has been modified by several states and written into bills for legislative action. While this plan did break with established insurance practice, it did not go far enough. A two-tiered system of reparations is not conducive to reducing costs, nor is it fair to the accident victim. Victims who are seriously hurt in auto accidents would still be subject to the inequities of negligence laws. Because most of the proposals contained in the Basic Protection Plan occur in other plans which will be discussed, we will reserve comment for these plans.

THE CONNECTICUT PLAN

Perhaps no automobile-insurance reform plan has given in to the power of vested interests more than that proposed by the Connecticut Insurance Department. The Connecticut plan, better known as the Cotter Plan after Commissioner William R. Cotter, is a tribute to the power of the insurers and the lawyers whose interests are so carefully protected in the provisions of the plan.

The Cotter Plan is not a no-fault system; it is, however, designed to increase the scope of protection to the accident victim. Unfortunately, the increased protection

156

will only serve to increase rates. The principal provisions of the Cotter Plan are as follows:

1. Medical and hospital coverage of up to a $2,000 limit, and disability coverage of 85 percent of gross income lost, commencing 30 days after the accident and continuing for 52 weeks, subject to a maximum of $500 per month, or a total of $6,000. These payments will be made regardless of fault. The insurance companies will decide among themselves, or through an intercompany panel, who was at fault, and the companies will reimburse each other accordingly.

2. For any small claim under $3,000 an arbitration board consisting of three lawyers is proposed. The decision of the board will not be final, allowing an appeals procedure for dissatisfied claimants or insurers. If any claim is disallowed, the claimant or his lawyer must pay the costs of the arbitration proceedings.

3. Any amounts paid by the insurers would be declared in any subsequent court action concerning the same accident, but only after the court has delivered its verdict. The payments made would be deducted from any amount allowed by the court.

4. Contributory negligence would be replaced with a comparative-negligence law. Contributory negligence allows that if any party in a legal proceeding is at fault, no matter how slightly, this contributory negligence would be cause to deny any reparations or damages. Under a comparative-negligence law, the court would decide the degree of negligence involved for each party, if any, and reparations and damages would be allowed according to this degree of negligence. Seven states have adopted the comparative-negligence system in this country.

5. Lawyers' contingency fees would be limited to 25 percent of the money collected by a claimant em-

ploying his services. The Cotter Plan also allows under certain conditions that the lawyer can petition the court for a higher fee.

6. Cancellations would be restricted to nonpayment of premiums, loss or revocation of driver's license, or automobile registration. The insurers would not be prohibited from failing to renew a policy. The only requirement would be 20 days' notice of intent to nonrenew.

7. Property damage would be settled separately from bodily injury arising out of the same accident where settlement is delayed.

8. Standards would be adopted for measuring pain and suffering. If hospital and medical expenses amounted to $500 or less, an award of up to 50 percent would be paid to the claimant of this loss. Medical expense in excess of $500 would allow an award of 100 percent of the medical expense. Awards of more than these amounts would be paid for death, disfigurement, dismemberment, or permanent impairment. These additional awards would be allowed after medical authorities demonstrated that these additional amounts would justly compensate the victim.

The Cotter Plan is not really an automobile-insurance reform system at all. What it actually accomplishes is an accommodation to the insurers and the legal fraternity, with the least possible disruption of the present system. If any plan is to make accommodations, it is to the insured. Not that the insurers should be treated unfairly; they should not. If the insurers are to offer reliable and extended continuity of service and benefits, they must be allowed a reasonable profit. But any plan reforming the present system can be fair to the insurers while offering the policyholders a humane, just, and genuine program of

158

benefits. The insurers are aware that change is needed, and the hope is that an equitable solution can be found. It is the state legislators and trial lawyers' associations that oppose any comprehensive reform bill, including a no-fault system.

Compulsory arbitration for disputed claims under $3,000 serves to impose a burden on the indigent claimant. If a claimant is to appeal a decision not in his favor, he must pay the arbitration costs within 20 days of the decision. In addition, his appeal must be financed at his own expense, because it is doubtful that an attorney would handle the case after an unfavorable decision from the arbitration board. It is doubtful, too, that an attorney would handle the case on a contingency basis considering the small amount of money involved. Proponents of the arbitration proceeding argue that it will reduce court congestion considerably. The truth is that very small claims never go to court at all. The insurers are certainly not going to pay beyond what they would ordinarily have paid under the present system, and under the present system the small claimant is paid very well not to go to court. It will only be the poor, who cannot fight back, who will be taken advantage of and will lose in arbitration proceedings.

The overlay of an advance-payment plan on the present tort reparations system can only increase inefficiencies and add to the administrative costs for the insurers. This cost will have to be assumed by the policyholders through increased premium rates.

One of the most thoughtless impositions on the policy-holders will be the automatic pain-and-suffering awards. It amounts to an open invitation to motorists to collect some easy money. There is no reason why any individual involved in an auto accident, after having his medical needs and wage losses compensated, should be handed a gift of

50 or 100 percent of his medical losses. This money serves no useful purpose when it is used as a gift; hard-earned premium dollars should be dispensed far more judiciously. The plan will certainly encourage inflated medical claims. Dishonest claimants coupled with unscrupulous doctors could drive up these costs beyond reason.

Fortunately for the motorists of Connecticut, the Cotter Plan was defeated. The problem is that other states will try to force this plan on their motorists, and the plan will probably be passed into law in a few states. The American Mutual Insurance Alliance is backing this plan and is hoping that many states will adopt it.

FIRST PARTY
MEDICAL INSURANCE

Under the present system of accident reparation, a victim is paid by his insurer even though he may have already collected from a collateral source for the same injury or for wage loss. In 1970, insurers paid approximately $484 million to claimants in duplicate benefits. This duplication of benefits is costly and unnecessary, but to eliminate the practice poses many problems. At least 56 percent of the motoring public has some form of collateral insurance. The sources of these benefits are Blue Cross- and Blue Shield-type plans, workmen's compensation, and wage-loss insurance plans. Sick-pay benefits paid by employers may be counted here as well.

If we allow the practice to continue, it will only add a burden to the already high liability rates for bodily-injury insurance. If we eliminate the duplication under a no-fault plan, there will be minor problems to solve such as the elimination of delay between the collateral insurer's exhaustion of benefits and the assumption of payments by the auto insurer.

The discussion here, however, centers around the present system. Insurers now offer a medical-payments coverage of between $500 and $5,000 on a first-party basis. This means that, should the insured be injured in connection with an automobile—whether it be a traffic accident or the hood falling on some unfortunate's head—the insurer will pay the medical costs up to the insured's limits regardless of fault.

Under the standard liability coverage, the motorist is insured if someone else is injured and seeks compensation from him, and the insurer must pay if its insured is proved to be at fault. We have seen how contributory negligence disallows a claimant from any compensation regardless of the circumstances. If this person has no other form of insurance, he must pay for his medical expenses out of his own pocket. Frequently, there is nothing in the pocket.

Even if the insured, under circumstances of contributory negligence, had only a $500 auto medical policy, that is all the insurer would pay. Medical costs today are extremely high, and the $500 would not go very far in paying for medical expenses arising out of a serious injury. Regardless of the circumstances, we must look at collateral sources of payment in a social context. There is no justification for an accident victim to be paid twice for the same injuries. But there is justification in having the victims, all victims, compensated for their auto-accident injuries regardless of fault.

It is perhaps a little naïve to expect that no-fault insurance will be adopted by every state in the near future. We can, however, look to our states to make auto medical policies compulsory, with minimum limits of at least $5,000. In addition, options could be offered at higher rates for higher coverage. The states could further legislate that accident and health insurers be prohibited from insuring anyone for auto injuries. This would enable these insurers to lower their rates, secure in the knowledge that they would not be liable for auto-accident victims. Nonmotorists would also benefit in that their rates would no longer be influenced by automobile-accident losses.

We must recognize that by internalizing accident costs we will not be saving any money for the motorists. The $484 million will still have to be paid by the insurers. The justification is that all accident victims would be paid for injuries arising out of traffic accidents regardless of fault. The insurance premiums paid to these collateral insurers would be substantially decreased, since they would not have to pay that portion of the $484 million that was paid to auto-accident victims.

SOCIAL SECURITY BENEFITS

The present Social Security Administration is a model of efficiency. For every $1 paid in, the administration pays out 95 cents. It is possible to theorize that, if the insurers and the state legislatures do not pass meaningful legislation for either no-fault plans or at least auto medical compulsory insurance, the federal government will have to do something about the situation. There are too many victims today uncompensated, and many who receive a pittance of their actual net economic losses from the present system.

It is not inconceivable that the Social Security Administration could be given the power to administer a national auto medical insurance plan. The organization is there, the system is there, and it is an excellent one. Why could we not have this solution to our problems with accident reparation? It would cost less than any other plan now under consideration and certainly far less than any plan under the present system.

NATIONAL HEALTH INSURANCE TO REPLACE AUTO BODILY INJURY INSURANCE?

The United States is the only major industrialized nation that does not have some form of national health service for its citizens. We also spend more money on health care than any other nation. In 1950, national health expenditures amounted to $12.9 billion. In 1970 the national health bill came to $63 billion; this makes health care the fastest-growing business in the country. And make no mistake, health care is a business.

Our hospital equipment and laboratories are the envy of the world. We can treat the most exotic diseases, surmount some of the foremost medical challenges, but yet we rank fourteenth in infant mortality in the world, eighteenth in life expectancy for men, and eleventh in life expectancy for women. One out of every four persons receiving in-hospital treatment does not belong in a hospital. Our knife-happy physicians perform twice as much surgery as other nations with superior health care.

Private health insurers have learned something from the auto insurers—risk selection. The young and healthy citizens can get insurance at reasonable prices, but the old and the sick must often pay exorbitant rates.

Any new plan that is designed to do away with abuses in the current health situation is strongly opposed by most of the nation's 313,000 active physicians. Doctors are responsible for the current situation; they are the ones who diagnose, treat, prescribe, operate, and commit to hospitals. They are partially responsible for high hospital

163

costs, and they certainly are responsible for the increase of 95 percent in doctors' fees that has occurred in the last 10 years. There are no color lines, income differences, or age requirements for sickness. Disease can strike anyone.

On January 25, 1971, 23 Senators introduced a health-care bill to the Senate. The bill would do away with Medicaid and Medicare and replace them with a system of national health insurance. Senator Edward M. Kennedy summarized the principal features of the bill as follows:

The National Health Insurance Plan would provide a system of comprehensive national health insurance in the United States, capable of bringing the same quality of health care to every man, woman, and child in the nation. It would also use the insurance program as a lever to bring about major improvements in the organization and de-livery of health care.

Every individual residing in the United States would be eligible. There would be no requirement of past individual contributions, as in Social Security, or a means test, as in Medicaid.

The program would cover all health services for the prevention and early detection of disease, the care and treatment of illness, and major medical rehabilitation. There would be no cut-off dates, no coinsurance, no waiting periods, and no deductibles. The only exceptions would be certain expenses for nursing-home care, adult dental care, psychiatric care, and some drugs.

All doctors and hospital expenses would be paid directly by the program. Individuals would not be charged for national health insurance services.

The programs would be paid for out of a health security trust fund, composed as follows:

40 percent from general tax receipts
35 percent from a 3.5 percent payroll tax (employers)

25 percent from a tax of 2.1 percent on employees' wages and individual income, up to $15,000 a year. The employer may pay all or part of its employees' tax and would be expected to preserve obligations under existing collective bargaining.

The program would be administered by a five-member panel of the Health Security Board in the Department of Health, Education and Welfare, which will establish policy, standards, and regulations for the program.

Five percent of the trust fund will go into programs to improve the health system, especially in the areas of manpower, innovative services, and facilities.

As is obvious, this plan is not a socialized-medicine scheme but a plan whereby every man, woman, and child will receive complete medical care, and pay for it. If such a plan were passed, the need for auto bodily-injury insurance would be eliminated. This discussion does not pretend to offer solutions to far-reaching social problems. However, we have established that the problems of the auto-insurance industry are in need of solution, and that solution can take many forms.

We must look at every possibility before we make any decisions as to plans that will be federally controlled and national in scope. If we are to accept the National Health Insurance Plan, we must be positive that the second, third, or even fourth order of effects will not be disastrous. A program that solves one problem only to create an even larger problem is not a solution. We need a system of national health insurance, and eventually we will have one. This plan appears to merit our consideration.

UNIFORM MOTOR VEHICLE
INSURANCE ACT

The federal government is not to be overlooked in the race to reform our automobile-insurance system. Senator Hart's Subcommittee on Antitrust and Monopoly started an investigation of the present system in 1967. The results of this investigation led to four proposals which were presented to the Congress in September of 1970. They were the Uniform Motor Vehicle Insurance Act, the Motor Vehicle Group Insurance Act, the Motor Vehicle Information Act, and an amendment to the Internal Revenue Act of 1954. Each of these legislative proposals is of significant interest to the motoring public, and an explanation of each follows:

The Uniform Motor Vehicle Insurance Act is modeled after the New York No-Fault Plan, although there are several differences. Basically the act would provide a no-fault reparations system for victims of automobile accidents. In addition, it provides that motorists would be liable for "catastrophic harm" under a fault determination. The act defines catastrophic harm as a bodily injury (including death at any time as a result of injury) which results in a permanent or partial loss of use of a bodily member or bodily function. It also includes disfigurement. For instance, if an insured was involved in an accident where he lost a limb, and the driver of the other car was clearly at fault, the victim's basic insurance would cover wage loss for 30 months. The wage-loss provision provides that the victim's wages, less taxes, would be paid up to $1,000 per month.

The basic coverage would also provide payments for all medical expenses without limit including prosthetic services. The victim could undergo physical therapy as soon as he was able, followed by occupational therapy in a new

occupation which would also be paid by his insu

All of these benefits would be provided regardless
fault under the basic policy. The victim, however, becau
he had lost a limb, would be allowed to sue the neglige
driver under the catastrophic-harm provision of the a
The victim might estimate that over the course of his wo
life, the loss of his limb, due to the other driver
negligence, would cost him $15,000. The victim coul
then sue for that amount. Catastrophic harm is the onl
exception to the no-fault provisions of the act.

The act requires that any collateral benefits, such a
Blue Cross and Blue Shield, sick pay, or any other type o
wage insurance, be paid before the victim's insurer would
pay benefits under the basic policy.

Every licensed driver would be eligible for insurance,
and insurance policies could not be canceled, nor could the
insurer fail to renew a policy unless the insured had his
license suspended or failed to pay his premium.

Insurance would be compulsory in each state and would
be a precondition for using the public streets.

All auto insurers and rating bureaus would be required
to submit to the Secretary of Transportation, at least every
six months, and a complete breakdown of policy costs.
These prices would be published for the public's use in
comparing costs.

Death benefits would be payable up to a maximum of
$30,000.

The act would set up an assigned-claims plan. Each state
would organize its insurers into a pool. If an insurer
became insolvent, or if a hit-and-run accident occurred in
which a pedestrian was injured, or if there were an
accident where no insurance benefits were applicable,
insurers in the pool would be required to absorb the claims
costs according to their gross business. For instance, a
company writing $10 million yearly in premiums would

not be expected to bear a share of these claims equal to a company, such as Allstate, which would write perhaps $50 million in the same state.

Periodic payments for all medical, hospital, surgical, professional nursing, and prosthetic services, as well as physical and occupational therapy, and all necessary expenses would be made by the insurers. If an insurer does not make a payment within 30 days, the act provides that the insurer be penalized at an interest rate of 20 percent on the payment.

Wage loss would be paid by the insurers for earnings that the victim would have made had he not been injured. A ceiling of $1,000 per month for 30 months would be paid exclusive of taxes.

These are the principal benefits under the act, and all of these would be provided under the basic liability coverage. In addition, the act allows for optional benefits. Catastrophic-harm insurance will be provided at minimum coverages of $50,000 for any one person and $300,000 for all persons in any single accident. The optional insurance may also include additional benefits for injury, death, property damage, or any other loss from motor-vehicle accidents. These optional benefits, however, are only offered in excess of standard liability policies.

MOTOR VEHICLE GROUP INSURANCE ACT

In addition to the rate reductions that almost certainly would follow the passage of the Uniform Motor Vehicle Insurance Act, the Motor Vehicle Group Insurance Act will benefit many drivers. Estimates of 15 percent have been projected in additional rate savings under group purchasing of automobile insurance. Senator Hart's

proposed legislation would allow any group not formed for the specific purpose of purchasing insurance to purchase a master policy or operating agreement from an insurer.

The group act would function similarly to group hospitalization plans like Blue Cross and Blue Shield. Policies would be issued regardless of risk, at one average rate for the group. Each year's rate would be based on the previous year's loss experience.

Employers could offer auto insurance under the payroll deduction plan, and they could participate on a shared-cost basis, as many of them do under hospitalization insurance. The employer could then negotiate with the insurers for a group contract. The group act is only enforceable for those companies operating on an interstate basis. Insurers domiciled in only one state would not be forced to comply with the group-act provisions. States would not be allowed to impose penalties or restrictions on any insurer legally allowed to offer group insurance.

In order that employers might take advantage of the group plan, through payroll deductions, and participate in the cost sharing, Senator Hart proposed an amendment to the Internal Revenue Act of 1954. This amendment would allow employers tax relief in the form of tax deductions on gross income for their contributions, through cost sharing, for group auto insurance.

MOTOR VEHICLE INFORMATION ACT

The Motor Vehicle Information Act is an amendment to the National Traffic and Motor Safety Act of 1966.

1. *The act would require rating of cars for relative susceptibility to damage and injury to occupants in low-speed conditions.* Senator Hart's subcommittee inves-

tigation showed that 75 percent of crash claims were under $200. In an auto-susceptibility test, four 1969 medium-priced sedans were crashed into a solid barrier at five miles per hour; the damage to each averaged $200. Autos can be manufactured to withstand impacts of 40 miles per hour into a solid barrier with no injury to the auto's passengers. A solid-barrier impact at 40 miles per hour is equivalent to two autos colliding at 75 miles per hour. Hart's bill would be the first step toward a much safer auto and a far less expensive one to repair.

There are two theories behind the rating of cars, the first being that cars with a low damage susceptibility could be given lower insurance rates by the insurers. The second theory is that the auto manufacturers should be forced into a competitive situation where they would have to produce safer cars.

The bill also requires a feasibility study for rating cars by the relative susceptibility of injury and death to passengers.

2. *The bill would strengthen vehicle inspection.* Inspection would be required before a vehicle could be sold to a consumer. This inspection would be performed by specially trained personnel in inspection stations in each state. The inspectors would not be allowed to work for any garage, service station, or mechanic's shop, thereby eliminating possible conflict of interest. Hart also proposed that consumers wishing to have a car inspected before purchasing it could use the facilities of the inspection station. The stations could also be used as diagnostic clinics so that consumers needing repairs would know exactly what was wrong with their automobiles.

3. *A uniform titling system would be established.* Titling laws increase the chances of stolen vehicles' recovery. States with titling laws recover some 85 percent of their

stolen cars. New York, without a law until March of 1971, recovered only 51 percent in 1970.

The Motor Vehicle Information Act will serve to strengthen the National Traffic and Motor Safety Act of 1966. A conservative estimate of $10 billion is spent annually in repairs to automobiles that are not needed, improperly repaired, or not done at all. Every motorist has been faced with the dilemma of leaving a car to be repaired and finding that the "funny noise in the muffler" turned out to be a $300 repair bill for the vague innards of the engine that just had to be repaired. A month later the motorist hears the "funny noise" again and takes the car back to the shop. This time the muffler is replaced at a cost of $100, and the motorist wonders how it happened. If he had inspected the muffler, he might have found the temporary patch that had been put on the first time he went into the shop and for which he paid $300.

Hart's proposed legislation is still in the formative stage. His insurance bills are designed to eliminate the present inequities in our insurance system. They would also serve to make future auto insurance much more reasonably priced. All four bills, however, face stiff opposition from Congress. It would be unreasonable to think that any of these bills would get out of committee unscathed. The problems of the automobile industry and the insurers are slated to become the No. I consumer issue for the next several years. It would also be naïve to think that some form of federal legislation will not come out of the Congress.

THE MASSACHUSETTS
NO-FAULT PLAN

Massachusetts has been an insurer's nightmare for years,

but for the policyholder it has been worse. With 2.5 million registered private automobiles, the state is first in liability-claims frequency and has the highest rates in the country. The state has had compulsory auto insurance for over 40 years, and this, the insurers are quick to point out, is the cause of much of their woe.

The history of the first no-fault plan to be passed in this country began in 1967, with State Representative Michael S. Dukarkis sponsoring a version of Keeton and O'Connell's Basic Protection Plan. Much to the surprise of everyone in the industry, the bill was passed by the House its first time out. In September of 1967, however, the industry and the trial-lawyers associations marshaled their resources and managed to defeat the bill in the Senate. An amended version of the bill was introduced to the House in late 1968 and failed to win a majority.

With the election of Francis W. Sargent to the governor's office and his eventual sponsorship of the no-fault plan, legislation was again introduced in the House in 1970. This time the bill was passed by the House, and then in the Senate an amendment was tacked on, through the efforts of the trial-lawyers association, to decrease all auto rates by 15 percent. The bill went back to the House where another amendment was introduced which was a severability clause. This allowed the governor to remove the rate decreases, or the insurers to take the issue to court, in order that they might be removed.

The bill was finally signed into law in August of 1970. One of the features of the new law called for noncancelable auto policies. This provision incensed the insurers, who called it a lifetime guarantee to the insured that their policies could never be canceled for any reason.

In November, the governor signed an emergency law abrogating several features of the original law. One of these was the noncancelable provision. This emergency law

172

amounted to a concession to the insurers so that they would have some basis for nonrenewal and for cancelations. The matter of the rate decreases was too hot an issue for the governor to change.

Several of the insurers, as a result, refused to write any more new policies in the state, or to renew any existing policies. These companies—Aetna Casualty, Employer-Commercial Union Companies, and Lumberman's Mutual—were adamant in their refusal to write policies unless the decreases were rescinded. However, not every decrease was distasteful to them. The insurers held that, *due to the no-fault plan*, rates on bodily injury could be reduced 15 percent. Their argument was with the decreases in auto property damage and auto physical damage. The attorney general of the Commonwealth of Massachusetts promptly labeled this action a conspiracy to fix prices, and held that these companies were acting in restraint of trade. The state further countered with the statement that the recalcitrant companies would not be allowed to write any kind of insurance in the state unless they complied with the new law. The insurers finally took the issue to the state Supreme Court and won a reversal on property-damage rates alone. Further action was announced for the other types of coverage as soon as the court would hear the cases, but, the insurers held bodily injury rates would remain at the 15 percent reduced level.

All of this, of course, was a political strategy. The governor had been put into an embarrassing political situation, and he could not afford to back down. The insurers played the issue for all it was worth, and the most astounding effect of the property-damage decrease reversal occurred the following day. State Insurance Commissioner C. Eugene Farnham announced a 38 percent *increase* in property-damage rates. No doubt the insurers are still chuckling over that one.

The basic features of the Massachusetts No-Fault Plan are as follows:

Accident victims will be reimbursed by their own insurers for medical and out-of-pocket expenses, up to a limit of $2,000, regardless of fault. A claimant will also be reimbursed for up to 75 percent of his previous year's wages. A plaintiff can recover damages for pain and suffering under negligence law if medical expenses exceed $500, or there is bone fracture, disfigurement, loss of limb, sight, or hearing.

Motorists in 1971, and in subsequent years, will be allowed a rate reduction of 2 percent for each year of accident-free driving up to a maximum of 10 percent. The maximum will then apply for as many years as the driver has no accidents.

Traffic violations will carry with them, in addition to fines paid the city or state, a surcharge on auto-insurance rates. These are 20 percent for speeding and 10 percent for any other moving violation. Drivers convicted of drunken driving or driving under the influence of drugs will be surcharged 100 percent of premium. In no case will a surcharge be in effect for more than five years.

Deductibles of $250, $500, $1,000, or $2,000 can be purchased in liability policies. The driver, or any other person riding in the insured's car, will forfeit the deductible in any claim against his insurer.

There will be some duplication of benefits allowed.

The provisions of the emergency law which amended the noncancelable feature of the original law are as follows:

For every policyholder aged 65 years or older, no insurance policy could be refused renewal unless the policyholder was convicted of a moving violation or had his driver's license suspended for more than 30 days. If a driver was ineligible for the merit system, due to accident involvement, or did not pay his premium, he could be refused renewal. In the case of a particular insurer, which refused to renew because of a general reduction in the volume of automobile insurance written, the insurance commissioner would have to pass on the validity of the reason for nonrenewal.

Persons under 65 years of age could be refused insurance if they violated any of the above provisions. The state further allowed that, for any cancellation other than for fraud or nonpayment of premium, the insurer would be required to accept an additional applicant under the assigned-risk plan.

The problem with the Massachusetts plan is that it does not go far enough in offering no-fault benefits. Because it is a two-tiered system, savings in premiums are necessarily lessened. Whenever an insurer must process some claims under a no-fault procedure, and some under a fault procedure, excessive costs are involved. Even Representative Dukarkis has voiced the opinion that the $500 limit on no-fault medical payments is too low. Allowing for the normal greed of lawyers, doctors, and claimants, the state might see many medical claims coming in at $501 allowing for negligence action. The provisions of the emergency law are shameful, because they have nullified what could have been a precedent-setting move to force insurers to issue noncancelable policies to all.

This plan has been worked into a final form, but it will take some time before we can see how the insurers and attorneys will interpret the new law and how they will implement it. In May of 1971, Governor Sargent claimed the new no-fault plan a success, noting a claim-frequency reduction of 38 percent over the previous year. Though this appears to be good news, it will not be until the system has been in effect for at least a year that any significance can be given to claim reductions. There is speculation that trial lawyers have been holding up some claims while awaiting further developments.

THE AMERICAN INSURANCE ASSOCIATION PLAN

The American Insurance Association (AIA) represents some 30 percent of the stock auto insurers. Companies like Aetna Insurance Company, Travelers, and Firemen's Fund are members. Aetna Insurance has been a strong supporter of no-fault as it is presented by the AIA, and is working vigorously for its adoption.

Basically, the AIA Plan is a comprehensive plan with some differences from the New York plan. These differences are an income level of $750 per month as the top reimbursible wage benefit. The second is the collateral-benefits portion of the plan. In the AIA Plan collateral benefits would not be subtracted from total benefits paid for economic loss. The AIA does provide that optional coverages for wage losses beyond the standard limits would be available, as would optional coverage for disfigurement or permanent disability.

THE NATIONAL ASSOCIATION OF INDEPENDENT INSURERS DUAL PROTECTION PLAN

In December of 1970 the largest insurers in the country came out with a proposal combining no-fault benefits with the right of further recovery under tort. The independent insurers include such giants as State Farm, Allstate, and Nationwide in their membership. The plan's provisions are as follows:

1. Broadening of auto-insurance policies to afford

176

basic immediate-pay coverage of at least $2,000 in medical-expense benefits and $6,000 in wage-loss benefits to all persons injured while riding in or struck by the insured car.

2. Required offering of catastrophic coverage to all policyholders and their families, extending the scope of the basic immediate-pay protection to at least $10,000 per person for medical expenses and wage loss, and $25,000 in death benefits.

3. Preservation of an innocent victim's right to recover damages from a wrongdoer, including economic losses beyond those afforded by the immediate-pay coverage, as well as reasonable compensation for noneconomic loss.

4. Streamlining the judicial process by providing special arbitration of small-claims procedures for quick economical disposition of all cases under $3,000.

5. Further minimizing the cost of the system by adopting standards governing the amounts recoverable for pain and suffering, and inconvenience in the less serious cases, and requiring that awards for wage loss be computed net of income taxes.

6. Court supervision of the lawyer's contingent-fee system in jurisdictions where it is not now regulated.

7. More stringent penalties for fraudulent claims.

8. Increased research and action to reduce the frequency and severity of accidents, to improve automobile design, and to cut auto-repair costs.

At first blush this plan suggests the possibility of a happy compromise between both systems. In fact, one wonders why the plan does not go all the way in offering no-fault benefits. At this writing, the final details of the Dual Protection Plan have not been published. It would

177

perhaps be unfair to criticize without this information. However, the plan is definitely a two-tiered system that will require the consumer to pay for the administration of two reparations systems.

The proposals are vague as to why an arbitration system would be necessary if no-fault benefits amounting to $8,000 are paid immediately to all parties regardless of fault. It would appear that this plan is expensive and that it would not do away with all of the problems in the present system.

PROSPECTS FOR CHANGE

The opponents of no-fault have drawn the battle lines and have proceeded to organize a vicious attack against it. The battle will not be confined to any one state, nor will the federal government fail to feel the effects of the campaign. So far their strategy has proved successful, with only one defeat in Massachusetts, but even here they were able to water down the no-fault provisions until they were virtually worthless. The real issue here is money, and the stakes are high.

The most vocal opponents are the trial-lawyers associations. These associations have for some time wrapped their real motives in cloaks of concern for the public welfare. The trial lawyers' arguments center around the illusory principles of right and wrong, and their opposition to no-fault is clearly defined in the October/November, 1970, issue of *Trial* magazine.* In this publication, the following hypothetical case is used as a basis for their position:

---

*A national legal news magazine, published by the American Trial Lawyers Association.

Assume a reckless, irresponsible driver crashes a red light, runs a stop light, or attempts to pass in a no-passing zone, and causes a violent accident. He mutilates the driver and passengers in a vehicle which was proceeding properly, and totally wrecks the car. Under the A.I.A. Plan (the no-fault plan of the American Insurance Association), the wrong driver is not at fault, nor is he liable. He is not responsible for the medical bills of his victims, nor for the repair bill or loss bill for the car. He cannot be sued, for any amount. The persons he injures can make no claim against him in any court.

In short, every traditional right of the innocent victim of a wrongdoer is totally abolished if the instrument of harm is a motor vehicle.

A prudent man, knowing he could never recover from the reckless driver under the no-liability plan, might wish to buy health and accident insurance to give himself and his family some protection.

This plan gives him no choice. He must buy, whether he wishes to or not. He will be compelled to buy from a private insurance company, at a cost dictated by the company to its captive market, a health and accident policy which contains a set schedule of benefits.

He will receive a percentage of his lost wages, providing he is earning any wages at the time, and providing he is not earning too much. There are upper limits on wage losses. Medical and hospital bills will be paid. Even though he may have full medical coverage from other sources he must buy the Plan's medical coverages.

He will recover nothing for the property damage to his car. He will recover nothing for loss of sight, loss of limb, disfigurement, disability or the agony of torn flesh.

The Plan requires each driver to carry a form of low-limit compulsory life insurance for himself and

179

his passengers, so that modest death benefits can be paid in the event of fatal injury.

The American Trial Lawyers has heard no arguments that the A.I.A. Plan is fair or just. Its proponents say it will be cheap. It should be. It would be even cheaper if the government furnished the Plan and eliminated a substantial part of the sales expense and the private profit.

The A.I.A. Plan is simply a form of Social Security for automobile occupants, with compulsory coverage regardless of individual responsibility or individual need.

All such systems can be operated more economically by government agencies. The American Trial Lawyers Association opposes the A.I.A. Plan, but adds that if such a scheme is to be imposed on the American public then it ought to be funded by the federal or state government and not mandated for the private benefit of the health and accident insurers.

What have they really said here? If a reckless driver crashes into another car and is at fault, that he is not responsible for his actions? The driver in this example is no different from the driver under the same circumstances in the present system. The driver who causes the accident does not pay; his insurer pays. What possible good would the right to sue do here?

At least under a comprehensive no-fault plan the accident victim *knows* that his medical and wage losses will be compensated, and there will be no delays, appearances in court, or a large attorney's fee to pay. The victim knows that he will not be cheated out of his compensation because of the vagaries of contributory negligence. We have seen that there are so many factors that can be involved in the determination of fault in an accident that the concept is no longer valid.

180

The ATLA's statement goes on to suggest that there is something wrong with compulsory automobile insurance, that it is or should be the right of every individual to determine whether he wants to provide for himself and for others. This sort of reasoning would be fine if we were to know that we would not have an accident, and if this were the case, there would be no need for insurance at all.

Another major point this statement makes is that an accident victim would "recover nothing for loss of sight, loss of limb, disfigurement, disability, or the agony of torn flesh." The writer of this statement is arguing his case as if he were in court, using the same sensational language—*i.e.*, the "agony of torn flesh." Dramatics may win the day in court, but they have no place in law journals.

A point of fact that the writer here seems to have overlooked or ignored is that the AIA Plan does provide a mechanism for making payments to persons who sustain permanent impairment or disfigurement in automobile accidents. The plan provides for optional additional insurance for permanent loss, and it would be readily available to motorists.

The last point here is that the trial lawyers claim that the AIA Plan is not a good one. Yet they suggest that if the plan were adopted by the government at either the state or federal level, it would not be so bad. The plan is either good or bad, and whether it is administered by the government or private insurance companies, its value will not change. It would appear that the trial lawyers do not know what they want in a system of auto insurance.

If we put aside all of the window dressing, we see that the trial lawyers do not want a no-fault insurance system, because they would lose a considerable amount of income. Some sources estimate that trial attorneys derive half of their income from auto-accident litigation as we have already indicated. The fight by the attorneys is logical and understandable. No one wants to lose half of his income, for any reason. But there are higher priorities here. We have thousands of accident victims who are unable to make any money at all, and who have been forced into suffering and deprivation because of the present system. It would seem far more justifiable that the trial lawyers lose half of their incomes in order that a much larger number of victims be compensated. It is even more evident that a comprehensive, no-fault system is the only way that the motoring public will be able to realize any decrease in rates or, at the worst, their stabilization.

The second level of opposition to no-fault comes from the insurers, agents, and from the legislators. The insurance industry is divided on the problem. Many of the large stock companies seem to favor some kind of no-fault scheme, and even the large mutuals have gone along with no-fault, as the National Association of Independent Insurers' no-fault plan indicates. But it is the small insurers who fear no-fault.

The reason is, some experts say, that the small mutual and stock companies fear the entry of the major life-insurance companies into the auto-insurance market. No-fault insurance lends itself to mass-merchandising methods, and life companies have developed an expertise in this area that could be brought into the auto-insurance industry. The small companies fear that they simply would not be able to compete with these large life companies.

The insurance agent is another thorn in the side of reform. Naturally, the issue is again income. If no-fault insurance is some 33 percent or more cheaper than present insurance, and if it is mass-merchandised, bringing about even greater premium reductions, the agents' income will be adversely affected. Again their opposition is logical and understandable. But we cannot allow thousands of accident victims to suffer, so that insurance agents will live high off policyholders.

Finally, we come to the most influential segment of the opposition—the legislators. We have shown how many state legislators are mere pawns in the hands of vested interests. The shame of it is that for the last 20 years these legislators have been deluged with mail from their constituents complaining about insurer practices and the failures of the present system. Yet, political considerations and their own vested interests have limited any effective legislation. We now have no-fault bills before the legislatures of 28 states and many more to come, but these same political hacks will stall, equivocate, and fight these bills to their legislative deaths if they are allowed to.

It is only when the public really understands what is involved, what the real issues are, and how it is in their best interests to bring about these changes, that these political shenanigans will become intolerable, and no-fault will become part of the law.

The purpose of this book has been to bring all of the issues into the open. In this way every motorist can be apprised of the entire auto-insurance system and can decide what he wants. There is no time left for equivocation, the decisions must be made now.

GLOSSARY

10/20/5: $10,000, $20,000, $5,000. See *Policy Limits.*

ADVANCE PAYMENT PLANS: Allowing a claimant to collect partial payments but only when liability is clear.

AGENCY COMPANY: An insurance company whose business is produced through a network of independent agents as distinguished from a direct-writing company whose business is produced by company employees.

AGENCY SYSTEM: System of producing business through a network of agents. Such agents have a contract to represent the company and are of three classes: local, regional, and general. These agents are compensated at different rates of commission. General agents have a greater responsibility than other kinds of agents.

AGENTS' BALANCES: Premium balances, less commission payable thereon, due from agents and brokers to the insurer.

ASSETS, ADMITTED: Assets stated at values permitted to be reported in the convention statement filed with the various state insurance departments.

ASSETS, NONADMITTED: Assets, or portions thereof, which are not permitted to be reported as admitted assets in the convention report filed with state insurance departments. Nonadmitted assets are specifically defined by the insurance laws of each state. Other assets, too, are not allowed as admitted assets. Major nonadmitted assets are excess of book over statement value of investments, agents' balances or uncollected premiums over three months due, furniture, fixtures, supplies, automobiles, etc.

ASSIGNED RISK POOLS: Arrangements by which bodily-injury and property-damage insurance can be obtained by persons who have been denied insurance through normal channels. Insurance obtained in this fashion is usually much more expensive than insurance obtained through normal channels.

BODILY-INJURY LIABILITY INSURANCE: This coverage applies when the policyholder's car injures or kills pedestrians, persons riding in other cars, or guests in his own car. It is in force as long as the insured car is driven by the policyholder, members of his immediate family, or others who drive the car with his permission. Care must be exercised here that there is no specific exclusion as to the use of the car by anyone other than the policyholder. Failure to observe this exclusion could result in nonpayment of a claim.

Under most policies, the policyholder and all relatives in his household are covered even while driving someone else's car, if they have the owner's permission. In some policies, if such a relative owns his own car, he must have his own policy, to be covered while driving someone else's car. When claims or legal action for damages for bodily injury are brought against the policyholder, the insurance company provides protection in the form of legal defense, and if the company agrees—or a court decides—that the policyholder is legally liable for the injury, his company will pay for the bodily-injury damages up to the limit of the policy. The policyholder should be cautioned here that the usual limits of 10/20/5 are inadequate. The minimum limits should be 25/50/10. It is extremely important that the policyholder realize that he is liable for any amounts of money exceeding his insured limit. This insurance does not cover the insured's own economic losses from bodily injuries and property damage. Such economic losses are compensated, if at all, by other insurance of the insured, by liability insurance of other parties in the loss-producing accident, or by other noninsurance sources of compensation. At this writing, 34 states have contributory-liability statutes. That is, if both drivers are in the slightest degree negligent in an accident, neither will collect from their bodily-injury insurance coverage. In the eight states with comparative-negligence statutes, the court will decide compensation according to the degree of negligence of each driver in the accident.

BODILY INJURY: Any injury involving bodily harm, including trauma.

BROKER: A licensed agent of the insured who buys insurance for his client from an insurance company. The compensation for his services consists of commissions paid to him by the insurance company. He is not an agent of a company, and the commission he receives is usually lower than that of an agent who legally represents the company.

CANCELLATION: A complete termination of an existing policy prior to normal expiration.

CAPITAL GAINS (CAPITAL LOSS): Profit or loss from the sale of a capital asset. A capital gain under federal tax laws may be short or long term. A short-term (6 months or less) capital gain is taxed at the regular corporate tax level.

187

A long-term capital gain is taxed at a maximum of 25 percent. Capital gains are also termed realized and unrealized. Realized capital gains are the proceeds of the sale of capital assets. Unrealized capital gains are those assets such as common stock or real estate which have appreciated in value but have not been sold to realize that value.

CASE RESERVE: The estimated value of future loss payments which are still to be made on an outstanding claim.

CLAIM OR LOSS EXPENSE: The expenses incurred in the investigation, adjustment, and settlement of losses. There are two types of claim or loss expenses: allocated and unallocated. However, there are no generally accepted definitions of these two terms. Allocated claims or loss expense is frequently considered to include expenses incurred in settling losses that can be attributed to specific losses, including such items as actual court costs, attorneys' fees, medical examinations, independent adjusters' fees, etc.

Unallocated claim or loss expense is frequently considered to include expenses, salaries of company loss-department employees, and all other direct and overhead expenses of the loss department.

CLAIMS OR LOSS EXPENSE: Death, injury, destruction, or damage in such a manner as to charge the insurer with a liability under the terms of a policy.

COLLISION PROTECTION: This coverage applies when the policyholder's car is damaged as a result of colliding with a vehicle, an object, or as a result of turning over. Damages are paid by the insurer regardless of who is at fault. Most collision insurance is sold with a $50 or $100 deductible feature. This means that the car owner sustains the loss of the first $50 or $100 of damage to his car in any one collision, and the insurer agrees to pay the remainder. Collision insurance does not cover injury to people or the property of others.

COMMON STOCK: Securities which represent an ownership interest in a corporation.

COMPREHENSIVE PHYSICAL DAMAGE INSURANCE: Under this coverage the insurance company pays the policyholder for loss resulting from damage to his car caused by falling objects, fire, theft or larceny, missiles, explosion, earthquake, windstorm, hail, water, flood, vandalism, riot or civil commotion, or collision with bird or animal. This insurance does not cover damage resulting from collision with another car or objects. Cracked or broken glass is also covered. This type of coverage has been especially misleading to some policyholders. The term "comprehensive" is only comprehensive insofar as it is outlined in the policy. The important point to remember under this form of coverage is that damages caused in a collision with another car are not covered in this policy. Claims for damages to private property are not covered as well.

CONGLOMERATES: A corporation that manufactures something or provides a service and in turn acquires companies in diverse fields, *i.e.*, aerospace, motion pictures, publishing, insurance. A conglomerate is distinguishable from a holding company only in that the holding company does not or may not provide a service or manufacture a product. See *Holding Company.*

CONTINGENCY RESERVES: Funds allocated for investment losses, catastrophes, bad debts, etc.

CONVERTIBLE: Bonds, debentures, or preferred stock which can be converted into common stock or another security, usually of the same company, in accordance with the terms of the issue.

DEBENTURES: The unsecured bonds backed by the general credit of a company, bearing interest at a specified rate with a set maturity.

DIRECT WRITING COMPANY, or DIRECT WRITER: An insurance company whose business is produced by company employees as distinguished from an agency company whose business is produced by agents.

DOWNSTREAM HOLDING COMPANY: A corporate device whereby a subsidiary company owned and controlled by the parent company forms a holding company.

EARNED PREMIUM: The pro-rata portion of the premium applicable to the expired period of the policy.

ENDORSEMENT: Documentary evidence of a change in an existing policy.

EQUITY IN THE UNEARNED PREMIUM RESERVE: Prepaid acquisition expenses applicable to unearned premiums. Pursuant to accounting practices prescribed for insurance companies, premiums are recorded as earned ratably over the terms of the policies issued, although related commissions, premium taxes, and other acquisition expenses are charged to income as incurred. This departure from the basic accounting concept of matching income and expense results in an equity in unearned premiums at any given date to the extent of the prepaid acquisition expenses applicable to such unearned premiums. There is another concept concerning the equity in the unearned premiums reserve, based on the premise that the unearned premium reserve exceeds the amount required to pay future losses and expenses on all unexpired policies; under this concept any unanticipated profit on the runoff of the unexpired policies is included in the equity.

FAULT: The legal determination of negligence in an accident.

FIRST PARTY CLAIMS: The process by which a claimant negotiates with his own insurer, without regard to fault, for a settlement. Collision insurance is first-party insurance. Third-party insurance, or liability insurance (bodily injury or property damage), is a process in which the claimant sues an insurer other than his own with regard to fault or negligence, for damages resulting from an automobile accident.

GENERAL DAMAGES: See *Pain and Suffering.*

HAZARD: The risk or peril or source of risk insured against, though in a strict technical sense each would have a slightly different meaning to the insurer.

HOLDING COMPANIES: Corporate device in which the corporate entity owns (holds) other companies.

INCURRED LOSS RATIO: Ratio calculated by dividing incurred losses by earned premiums.

INCURRED LOSSES (CLAIMS): Losses paid or unpaid for which the company has become liable during the period. Incurred losses for a period are calculated by adding unpaid losses at the end of a period to losses paid during the period and subtracting unpaid losses at the beginning of the period.

INDEMNIFY: To protect against possible damage, legal suit, or bodily injury.

INDEMNITY: Insurance or other security against possible damage, bodily injury, or legal suit.

INDEPENDENT RATING BUREAUS: Independent organizations which are concerned with the compilation of data involving all risks. This data is published with corresponding rates for each risk. Insurers subscribing to the rating bureaus use these rates as a basis for pricing individual policies. Insurers frequently have additional rating standards that are used in conjunction with the IRB rates.

INSTALLMENT PREMIUMS: Premiums payable on a periodic basis rather than in a lump sum.

INVESTMENT EXPENSES: According to the uniform expense regulations, all expenses incurred wholly or partially in connection with the investing of funds and the obtaining of investment income.

LIABILITY: Something for which one is liable. A person at fault in an accident is said to be liable for the accident. Liability insurance is the protection of the one who is liable from suits by others.

LINE: Type of insurance.

LOSS ADJUSTMENT EXPENSE: See *Claims or Loss Expense.*

LOSS RATIOS: The relationship between losses and premiums. Two ratios in common use are paid-loss ratio, which is the paid losses divided by earned premiums, and incurred-loss ratio, which is the incurred loss divided by the earned premium.

MEDICAL PAYMENTS INSURANCE: Under this coverage, the insurance company agrees to pay, up to the limit of the policy (usually $500 to $5,000), medical expenses resulting from accidental injury or funeral expenses in case of death. The coverage applies to the policyholder and his immediate family, whether in their own car or someone else's or if struck while walking. It applies to guests while they are occupying the policyholder's automobile. Payment is made regardless of who is at fault.

MUTUAL INSURER: A cooperative nonprofit association of persons in a corporation whose purpose is to insure themselves against risk.

NEGLIGENCE LAW: A standard whereby a person's actions are measured against what a hypothetical reasonable man would have done under the circumstances. A group of laws having their precedent in ancient common law.

NONCANCELLATION CLAUSE: Guarantee against termination of insurance, except for failure to pay premiums or revocation of a driving permit. Some insurers extend restrictions to include merit ratings and age in denying insurance renewals.

PAIN AND SUFFERING (GENERAL DAMAGES): A payment made by an insurer to accident victims for losses beyond economic loss.

PHYSICAL DAMAGE: See *Bodily-Injury Liability Insurance*.

POLICYHOLDER'S SURPLUS: The total capital funds as shown on the annual statement. Consists of capital, if any, unassigned funds (surplus), and any special surplus funds (contingency funds) which are not in the nature of liabilities.

POLICY LIMITS: Ten thousand dollars is the insurable limit for any one individual in an accident, and $20,000 the total amount of liability of all persons in one accident. The $5,000 applies to property damage. Much higher coverage is available and should be considered if the motorist has considerable assets to protect.

PREFERRED STOCKS: A class of stock with a claim on the company's earnings before payment may be made on the common stock and usually entitled to a priority over common stock if the company liquidates. This stock is usually entitled to dividends at a specified rate—when declared by the company's board of directors and before payment of a dividend on the common stock—depending on the terms of the issue.

PREMIUM: The amount of money paid for an insurance policy.

PREMIUM TAXES: Taxes levied, at rates varying from 1.5 percent to 4 percent, on premiums written in the various states.

PRICE-EARNINGS RATIO: The current market price of a share of stock divided by earnings per share for a 12-month period. For example, a stock selling for $200 a share and earnings of $10 a share is said to be selling at a price-earnings ratio of 20 to 1.

PRINCIPAL AMOUNT: Face or par amount of a security.

PROPERTY AND CASUALTY INSURER: Years ago home and accident insurance was known as property and casualty insurance. When the automobile came along, it too was considered to be property and casualty business. Many companies still retain the wording in their company names. Today the term "liability insurers" is more widely used.

PROPERTY DAMAGE LIABILITY INSURANCE: This coverage applies when the policyholder's car damages the property of others. More often than not the property is

194

another car. But this type of insurance also covers damage to other properties such as buildings, lamp posts, telephone poles, or trees. It does not cover damage to the policyholder's own car. The coverage is in force as long as the car is driven by the policyholder, members of his family, or others who drive the car with the owner's permission. The policyholder and members of his immediate family are covered while driving someone else's car if they have the owner's permission. When claims or suits for damage to property are brought against the policyholder, his insurance company provides protection in the form of legal defense, and if the company agrees—or a court decides—that the policyholder is legally liable for the damage, his company will pay the property damage up to the limits of the policy.

PROTECTION AGAINST UNINSURED MOTORISTS: This coverage applies to bodily injuries for which an uninsured motorist, or a hit-and-run driver, is legally liable. It applies to the policyholder and his family whether occupying their own car or someone else's or while walking. The coverage also applies to guests occupying the policyholder's car. The insurance company agrees to pay damages to injured persons to the same extent that it would if it had carried insurance on the uninsured or unknown motorist. It also includes damage to the policyholder's own car caused by an uninsured motorist. The uninsured-motorist endorsement is now available in all 50 states, the District of Columbia, and Puerto Rico. In 44 states, there is some measure of compulsion in acceptance of this coverage. Since 1961, this coverage has been expanded to include protection against insolvency of the insurance company that insures the person legally liable for the accident. This expanded coverage is meaningless in some states as the insolvent insurer has to be liquidated by the state. This process can take as long as 18 years, and the claimant could wait that long for a settlement.

REALIZED GAINS: See *Capital Gains.*

REINSURANCE: Insurance. Insurance companies insure themselves against possible unexpected losses with companies specializing in this field called reinsurers. Lloyds of London is the largest reinsurer in the world.

SPECIAL RISK CLASSIFICATIONS: Provide insurance at high rates for drivers who, because of disabilities or other factors, cannot qualify for normal rates.

STATUTORY: Relating to the laws of the federal or state governments enacted by legislatures.

STATUTORY LOSS RESERVES: The amount by which reserves required by law on bodily-injury and workmen's-compensation losses exceed the case basis loss and loss expense reserves carried by a company for such losses.

STATUTORY SURPLUS: Amount of money required by law of insurance companies for a specific line of insurance before policies can be written.

STOCK COMPANIES: Corporations organized for a profit to offer insurance against various risks.

STOCK WARRANTS: See *Warrants.*

STUDENT DISCOUNTS: Discounts allowed students taking driver-education courses.

SUBROGATION: The statutory or legal right of an insurer to recover from a third party who is wholly or partially responsible for a loss paid by the insurer under the terms of the policy. For example, when an insurer has paid the insured for loss sustained to his automobile as a result of a collision, the insurer may collect through the process of subrogation from the person whose automobile caused the damage.

TENDER OFFER: A device used by a company to gain control of another company or to simplify the corporate structure of the company making the tender. It is the offer to acquire a security owned by a shareholder and can be paid for with the exchange of stock, a combination of securities, or cash.

UNEARNED PREMIUMS: The pro-rata portion of the premium in force applicable to the unexpired portion of the policy term.

UNEARNED PREMIUM RESERVE: The estimated aggregate amount an insurer would be obligated to pay policyholders as return premiums for the unexpired term of their policies, if it should cancel every policy in force.

UNDERWRITING: The assumption of risk for designated loss or damage on consideration of receiving a premium. Usually also considered to embrace the determination of the acceptability of risks to be insured and of the proper premium to be charged.

UNREALIZED CAPITAL GAINS: See *Capital Gains.*

UPSTREAM HOLDING COMPANY: A holding company that controls the stock of the parent company.

WARRANTS: Certificates of promise to the buyers that they can purchase securities at a certain price and usually within a specified length of time.

BIBLIOGRAPHY

The following list of publications is offered for the individual desiring more information on the auto-insurance industry:

"Accidents, Money and the Law," Marc A. Franklin, Robert H. Chanin, Irving Mark, *Columbia Law Review*, Vol. 61, No. 1 (January 1961).

After Cars Crash, Robert E. Keeton and Jeffrey O'Connell. Homewood, Illinois: Dow-Jones-Irwin Co., 1967.

Actuarial Report on the Adequacy of the Costing of the American Insurance Association's "Complete Personal Protection Automobile Insurance Plan," prepared by the Actuarial Committee of the American Mutual Insurance Alliance, Chicago, Ill., 1969.

Automobile Insurance Study, A report by the staff of the Antitrust Subcommittee of the Committee of the Judiciary, House of Representatives. Washington, D.C.: U.S. Government Printing Office, 1967.

Basis of Rising Insurance Cost: Mathematica, Inc., Princeton, New Jersey, May, 1969.

Biography of an Idea, John Bainbridge. Garden City, N.Y.: Doubleday, 1952.

Competition, Regulation and the Public Interest in Non-Life Insurance, Roy F. Hensley. Berkeley and Los Angeles, University of California Press, 1962.

Crisis in Car Insurance, Robert E. Keeton, Jeffrey O'Connell, John H. McCord. Urbana, Ill.: University of Illinois Press, 1968.

Department of Transportation Automobile Insurance and Compensation Studies: U.S. Government Printing Office, Washington, D.C.

A Study of Assigned Risk Plans: Dennis P. Reinmuth, Associate Professor of Insurance, University of Michigan; Gary K. Stone, Associate Professor of Insurance, Michigan State University, August, 1970.

An Analysis of Complaints in Selected Automobile Insurance Markets: Douglas Olson, Ph.D., Asst. Professor of Insurance, University of Penn., assisted by August Ralston, Asst. Professor of Finance, Valparaiso University, July, 1970.

Automobile Accident Litigation: A report of the Federal Judicial Center. April, 1970.

Automobile Personal Injury Claims: Department of Transportation Staff Report, 2 Vols., July, 1970.

Causation, Culpability, and Deterrence in Highway Crashes: David Klein, Professor of Social Science and Human Development, Michigan State University, and Julian A. Waller, M.D., Professor of Community Medicine, University of Vermont College of Medicine, July, 1970.

Comparative Studies in Automobile Accident Compensation: Andre Tunc, Werner Pfennigstorf, Donald R. Harris, Jan Hellner, and Allen M. Linden. April, 1970.

Constitutional Problems in Automobile Accident Compensation Reform: Professor Joseph W. Bishop, Jr., Yale University; Professor Lindsey Cowan, Dean, University of Georgia Law School, April, 1970.

Driver Behavior and Accident Involvement: Implications for Tort Liability: Staff of Automobile Insurance and Compensation Study, Department of Transportation. October, 1970.

Economic Consequences of Automobile Accident Injuries: 2 Vols., Westat Research, Inc., Bureau of the Census. April, 1970.

Insolvencies Among Automobile Insurers: Douglas G. Olson, Ph.D., Assistant Professor of Insurance, University of Pennsylvania, July, 1970.

Insurance Accessibility for The Hard-To-Place Driver: Staff of the Division of Industry Analysis, Bureau of Economics, Federal Trade Commission, May, 1970.

Mass Marketing of Property and Liability Insurance: Spencer Kimball, Dean and Professor of Law, University of Wisconsin Law School; Herbert Denenberg, Loman Professor of Insurance, Wharton School of Finance and Commerce, University of Pennsylvania, June, 1970.

Motor Vehicle Assigned Risk Plans: William T. Hold, Associate Professor, Graduate School of Business, University of Texas at Austin, assisted by Harry P. Haiduk, University of Texas, August, 1970.

Price Variability in the Automobile Insurance Market: Calvin H. Brainard, Chairman, Department of Finance and Insurance, Stephan A. Carbine, Instructor, Department of Finance and Insurance, College of Business Administration, University of Rhode Island, August, 1970.

Public Attitudes Toward Auto Insurance: Staff Auto Insurance Compensation Study. September, 1970.

Public Attitudes Supplement to the Economic Consequences of Automobile Accident Injuries: Staff of Automobile and Insurance and Compensation Study, September, 1970.

Quantitative Models for Automobile Accidents and Insurance: Joseph Ferreira, Jr., Instructor, Massachusetts Institute of Technology, September, 1970.

Rehabilitation of Auto Accident Victims: John Henle, Vice-President, Columbus Ohio Area Chamber of Commerce, August, 1970.

Structural Trends and Conditions in the Automobile Insurance Industry: Staff of the Division of Industry Analysis, Bureau of Economics, Federal Trade Commission, April, 1970.

The Origin and Development of the Negligence Action: Wex S. Malone, Professor of Law, Louisiana State University; Fleming James, Professor of Law, Yale University; Cornelius J. Peck, Professor of Law, University of Washington; Dix W. Noel, Professor of Law, University of Tennessee, March, 1970.

Ethics and the Legal Profession: A Study of Social Control in the New York Bar, Jerome E. Carlin. 1963, unpublished report, Columbia University School of Law, Bureau of Applied Social Research.

Fundamentals of Fire and Casualty Insurance Strength, Roger Kenny. 4th ed. Dedham, Mass.: Kenny Insurance Studies, Dedham Press, 1968.

Insurance, Government and Social Policy, Spencer Kimball

and Herbert S. Denenberg. Irwin Series. Homewood, Illinois: Richard B. Irwin Inc., 1969.

Insurance Facts. Insurance Information Institute. New York, 1969.

Measurement of Profitability and Treatment of Investment Income in Property and Liability Insurance, Jon S. Hanson, Robert E. Dineen. Report by the National Association of Insurance Commissioners. June, 1970.

Perspective on Auto Insurance Reform. Testimony before New York State Joint Legislature. American Mutual Insurance Alliance. Chicago, Illinois, 1969.

Prices and Profits in the Property and Liability Insurance Industry. Report to American Insurance Association by the Arthur D. Little, Inc. Research Company. New York, November, 1967.

Report of the Special Committee to Study and Evaluate the Keeton-O'Connell Basic Protection Plan and Automobile Accident Reparations: American Insurance Association, September, 1968.

State of New York Insurance Department Reports:

Report of the Special Committee on Insurance Holding Companies: Oscar M. Ruebhausen, Chairman, Newell G. Alford, Jr., Samuel C. Cantor, Spencer L. Kimball, Stacy May, Oren Root. February, 1968.

The Public Interest Now in Property and Liability Insurance Regulation: Staff Report, January, 1969.

110th Annual Report of the New York State Insurance Department, 1968.

111th Annual Report of the New York State Insurance Department, 1969.

Automobile Insurance—For Whose Benefit?: Staff Report, 1970.

The Relationship Between Driving Records, Selected Personality Characteristics and Biographical Data of Traffic Offenders and Non-Offenders, Unpublished Ph.D. thesis, Earl Davis Heath, Ph.D. Center for Safety Education, New York University, 1967.

The Insurance Commissioner in the United States, Edwin W. Patterson. Cambridge, Mass.: Harvard University Press, 1927.

The Insurance Industry. Report on Hearings by the United States Senate Subcommittee on Antitrust and Monopoly of the Committee of the Judiciary: Vols. 12-15, 1965-1969.

Insurance: Rates, Rating Organizations and State Rate Regulations: Estes Kefauver, Tennessee, Chairman. August, 1961.

High-Risk Automobile Insurance, Part 12: Philip A. Hart, Michigan, Chairman. May, 1965.

Automobile Liability Insurance, Part 13: Philip A. Hart, Michigan, Chairman. June, 1968.

State Regulation for Solvency, Conglomerates and Insurance Companies and Case Study of One Nonrenewal: Philip A. Hart, Michigan, Chairman, March and May, 1969.

Unsafe at Any Speed, Ralph Nader. New York: Pocket Books, 1966.

Woodward and Fondiller, Inc., Report to National Association of Insurance Commissioners' Subcommittee to Study Reorganization and Public Information Matters, entitled "Study of Objectives, Operations and Organization of the N.A.I.C."